The Secret Door to Success:

Your Manifesting Blueprint

Kate Large
Florence Scovel Shinn

The Secret Door to Success: Your Manifesting Blueprint

Waiting in the Other Room Productions
WaitingInTheOtherRoom.com
SoulKisses.com
TheGameOfLifeMastery.com

ISBN 978-0-9826061-3-1

Printed in the United States of America

Manifesting what you want is simple:

Choose to be happy.

Fearlessly *DECIDE* what you want and Celebrate receiving.

Transform resistance fear energy to "Love or above."

Demand and execute Action Steps.

Prepare to receive.

Can it be this simple?

YES!

....it IS this simple!

Table of Contents

Introduction and Message from Kate Large

You Deserve to live a life filled with joy and happiness - it is your birthright!

There is ONE reason people create and live a less than joy filled life of suffering and worry instead of manifesting what will bring them joy, laughter and happiness in their lives.

They do not consciously know how to do anything different.

Everyone on the planet falls into one of these four categories:

Category #1

People who do not make a conscious decision of choosing what they want.

This person lives life subconsciously; allowing their subconscious beliefs to dictate the experience of their lives. These people live aimlessly adrift on the sea of life with no course of action that they stick to and are disappointed when they don't get what they want.

Category #2

People who make a conscious decision on what they want, but do NOT shift their energy to the joy that receiving what they want will give them.

This person maintains a status quo of manifesting over and over again things they do not want. They try to create a new or different experience from the same limiting energy of belief they created suffering with, and are disappointed when nothing changes.

Albert Einstein said it best: *"We can't solve problems by using the same kind of thinking we used when we created them."*

Category #3

People who consciously choose what they want, shift their energy to the joy of receiving, then when they're challenged by the fear filled, limiting subconscious thoughts and beliefs that blocked them from having what they want to start with, they throw up their hands, succumbing to defeat and claim it's too hard to be, have or do something better and they give up.

This person quits 5 minutes before the miracle occurs.

Category #4

People who consciously choose what they want, shift their energy to the joy of receiving what they want, and maintain that energy when there is no sign of receiving it. They maintain the joy energy of receipt, no matter what else is going on in their lives.

When resistance energy is revealed to them, they use their tools to face, disconnect and heal it. The resistance is fear filled, limiting subconscious thoughts and beliefs that have been hidden - sometimes for years. By processing through this energy of resistance, this person lives a happy, joy filled, miraculous life ===> their version of Heaven on Earth.

When beliefs of the subconscious are challenged, you're notified that your conscious and your subconscious are out of alignment when you feel the energy of resistance in your body.

Know that the resistance is a sign.

It's a Golden Opportunity to follow the breadcrumbs of uncomfortable resistant energy to its core and re-write the subconscious belief (neural pathway) to what your conscious and superconscious know to be true: You deserve to be, do or have whatever it is you wish to experience.

Which category describes your life?

The information in this book will show you how to overcome the human "need" to Give-Up!

The reality is this: You are The Master Creator of your life - you - you're the one doing the breathing in your body, you're the one creating your life experiences. And most importantly, YOU have the Power to create new experience, no matter what your life looks like in this moment.

Are you ready and willing to manifest a happier life? You're probably ready, but are you *truly willing?*

This is an experiential workbook to create your personal - customized - Manifesting Blueprint. A Manifesting Blueprint that you will use over and over again to manifest the joy and happiness you deserve!

Right now, you're powerfully creating your experience - you've created the good and the ugly. Now it's time to perfect manifesting what makes your heart sing with joy - consistently!

You are the Master Creator of your life - manifest something wonderful!

Implement these teachings to the best of your ability
and you will experience miraculous results!

This book includes *The Secret Door To Success* by Florence Scovel Shinn and uses her teachings to support and guide you to customize your personal, magical Manifesting Blueprint.

Are you unfamiliar with Florence's work?

For over 100 years the timeless, simple teachings of Florence Scovel Shinn has transformed the lives of MILLIONS of people, through her little book of wisdom: *The Game of Life and How to Play It!*

In the early 1900's she taught concepts of energetic vibration when the world was at war and fear was wide spread. People loved her teachings, but wanted them in written form.

In 1925 Florence self-published *The Game of Life and How to Play It* because no publisher of the time would touch it. As a result of her tenacity, Florence's teachings spread across the country and to other continents to support and guide people on how to miraculously change their lives no matter what their circumstances! And some of those circumstances were dire. The US suffered The Great Depression and the world was at war with World War I and World War II.

Today, I work, play and teach through Florence's spiritual energy - expanding her teachings into today's modern 21st century microwave society of "I want it now!"

The Secret Door to Success: Your Manifesting Blueprint includes Florence's book, *The Secret Door to Success,* a compilation of fourteen of her most powerful lectures. These lectures function as the energetic platform to structure your personal Manifesting Blueprint by revealing to you what has been holding you back.

You will learn to celebrate resistance for the Golden Opportunity it brings you, when you develop the eyes to see through the physical world illusion of despair and pain to "see" the limitless possibility that *IS* your birthright.

This workbook is designed to guide you step by step to process through your invisible, yet tangible blocks to customize your Personal Manifesting Blueprint. You may then use the blueprint over and over again to manifest what you want.

When you dive in deeply to the resources, guidance, insight and energy of this book, you WILL Transform-Your-Life!

We live in a microwave society. We want what we want and we want it now, and there's nothing wrong with that. This need within us results in manifesting quickly. However, what we manifest is the focus of our energy and many times that energy is less than love worry energy. As a result we manifest what we worry about instead of what we really want. Yikes!

We've perfected creating unhappy experiences through our worried, sad, depressed, desperate energy, as we've struggled with despair and feelings of being helpless. This ritual cycle establishes us as queens and kings of manifestation - Master Creators of manifesting, --- powerfully creating experiences we don't like.

Our mission here this lifetime on Mother Earth is to disconnect from the persuasive energy of fear and shift into the highest expression of the "love or above" vibration possible. From this higher vibratory force of love energy, you attract to you joy, happiness, peace, tranquility, serenity and harmony. When you maintain the highest vibration of love possible you will ultimately - inevitably - live *your version of Heaven on Earth* - whatever Heaven on Earth is for you.

...and the world around you transforms and ascends as well - even the soils of Mother Earth beneath your feet!

The energy and guidance of this book holds the power to transform your creation energy. When you implement the teachings, you will establish and perfect your power to manifest prosperity in all areas of your life - no matter what those areas look like in this moment!

What do you want to be, do or have? Do you want to experience a closer relationship with God? Do you want more money? Do you want a more loving relationship with your spouse or family? Do you want more joy and happiness in your life? Do you want a new house, new job or to own your own business? Do you want to travel? Do you want to receive more money?

Have you decided what you want?

If you're not willing to face your fears of the past that are revealed, and make
decisions to create a higher outcome, this book is not for you.

If you're not willing to work with the loving guidance of
Florence and your angels, this book is not for you.

However, if you're ready and *willing* to take serious action and reclaim your ability to fearlessly create the miraculous life that is your birthright, *this book was written Just-For-You!*

The basis for the magic of Florence's teachings is this:

Florence knew without a doubt that whatever her students wanted or needed, it was already made manifest at a higher plane of existence - it already had their name on it - no matter what it was. As a result, she easily held the space of knowing with unwavering faith that where there's a will, there is a way to manifest what brings the heart joy.

Florence's physical body passed away in 1940, but the energy of her spiritual essence lives on. This book is infused with Florence and my powerful loving energy of support. We, Florence and I, *know without doubt* that you <u>deserve</u> and are <u>worthy</u> to receive whatever it is you wish to be, do or have as your life experience - whatever brings your heart joy ==>*no matter what it is...*

The energetic container of this book and the information within the pages are powerful on their own, however, when you're ready to take your mastery to the next level, look into:

The GAME of LIFE Mastery Program

An extraordinary 60 day program designed to support you to transform your life. This program hosts a surplus of mastery tools, private Facebook community and life changing class modules to help you create your new life.

www.TheGameOfLifeMastery.com

and

The Secret Door to Success: Your Manifesting Blueprint MASTERMIND

This small, intimate, loving mastermind intensive opens the way to take manifesting what you want to the level of effortless brilliance!

www.SoulKisses.com/secret

www.MySecretDoorToSuccess.com

To learn more about Florence, our work together and how you can take your life to a New Superior Level of Mastery, go to the chapter titled: *More About Kate and Florence's Mastery Programs* at the end of this book.

Whenever you feel discouraged and doubt yourself, come back here and read this Statement of Truth:

YOU are a beautiful spiritual BE-ing of love and light and you deserve to live a life of joy, happiness and prosperity in all areas of your life - it is your birthright!

Florence and I hold you in the light of experiencing your greatest joy filled life - NOW!
So be it... and it is!

I invite you to click into the Soul Kisses website (www.SoulKisses.com) and get your Free Essential Mastery Tools. You'll meet your Worry Angel, receive guidance to shift your energy to love and access the power of gratitude - plus receive the Soul Kisses Spiritual Whispers newsletter - a newsletter that serves people in over 80 countries throughout Mother Earth!

These tools will provide you with extraordinary support as you navigate your life path. Click in and get yours - they're free! ---www.SoulKisses.com

You may also get more Manifesting Blueprint forms and other special goodies as my gift when you go to www.SoulKisses.com/success

In love and light,
Kate

How to Use This Book

If you're familiar with Florence Scovel Shinn's teachings, you know that when you read her books, *it is as if there are sections that were written just for you.*

After awhile, you come to realize that you can open the book at any page and you'll find information there that speaks to what is going on in your life in that exact moment that guides you to shift your energetic perception to create a higher outcome.

Plus you'll discover that her teachings are multifaceted. When you read the book again, at a later date - perhaps a week or months later, her teachings will speak to you in a deeper way than they did before. You'll also discover information you didn't see before. This happens because your awareness has expanded and you're at a higher vibration of understanding than you were the first time you read it. You'll find that this happens *Every Time* you read her books.

Florence's original book, *The Secret Door to Success,* is included here as a foundation of support to structure shifting your energy to customize your powerful personal Manifesting Blueprint. However, you'll find that the chapters are in a different order than the original book. They've been rearranged to support the flow of manifestation.

This book is presented in 6 sections with fourteen lectures or chapters from the original book. I recommend allowing yourself a few days or a week between moving on to the next lecture to allow your three levels of consciousness to manage the ascending flow of energy. The action steps after each lecture will support you to go deeper into how the energy of the teachings speak to you on the given day you read it.

WARNING: When you allow yourself to dive deeply into the energetic transformation this book holds for you, life will take on its own momentum of expansion, contraction and immediate transformation.

This book is designed to support you to shift and move a LOT of energy. Be gentle with yourself as your body acclimates to this energy shift. I recommend drinking lots of water and resting your body when it is tired. If you will nurture your body as well as your spiritual energy as you process through the book, transforming your life Will-Be-Easier!

Keep your Worry Angel Employed! It is not your job to worry! Your job is to ascend your energy to the highest vibration of love or above humanly possible - and that does not include worrying. (Didn't know you had a Worry Angel? Go to www.SoulKisses.com and get your free Essential Mastery Tools and you will meet your Worry Angel!)

Powerfully apply yourself as you read through each section allowing your consciousness to expand into the reality you wish to experience. From this expansion of consciousness, implement the Action Steps to create and customize your personal Manifesting Blueprint. Then execute your Manifesting Blueprint over and over again to manifest and live your most magnificent, joy filled life!

There are six sections:

Section I - Foundation for Success
Section II - Expecting and Receiving Miracles
Section III - Powerfully Manifest Through Your Energy
Section IV - The Shift from Trust to Knowing
Section V - Out-Picturing Beliefs as Prosperity
Section VI - Positioned for Success - Your New Life

The best way to use this book is to begin by being *willing to let go of your need to make manifesting what you want difficult*. It's the human condition to make things difficult - it's what we do, but it's time to put that behind you and create a new reality of existence.

The guidance and support of this book will escort you to overcome the "need" to give up when you run into obstacles. Namely, when the resistance of fear energy reveals itself in your body. Here you will learn what to do to stop the rollercoaster madness of trying to make changes to only give up when the "King-Pin" that blocks you shows up.

Right now, in this moment:

1. *Be* **WILLING** to accept your life as it is - whether you like your life or not. Accept what it is and be willing to let go of your need to beat yourself up about the things you're not in agreement with and have no control over.

Accepting what your life is doesn't mean you don't want something better or different, it simply releases you from the suffering, disappointment, despair and fear you may be experiencing.

When you accept your life as it is, you open the way to experience something new and different.

2. *Be* **WILLING** to release your fear of the unknown.

Many times you don't consciously choose to experience something new or different, because you're afraid. You may be afraid consciously or subconsciously. This fear stems from your doubt in your ability to create a new experience. You're afraid of the uncertainty - the unknown, so you don't do anything - you're frozen, paralyzed in fear - and many times you don't even know it. You think you're just struggling to survive and there isn't *"time"* to do anything else.

Consciously know there is "time."

The "unknown" is only unknown to your conscious state. Your higher self or superconscious is fully aware of all possibilities and works behind the scenes to guide you in the direction of the highest possible outcome.

Unfortunately when your subconscious is out of alignment with your conscious and superconscious, it does everything it can to "protect" you by stirring up the energy of fear when faced with the unknown - causing you to hesitate to rethink, agonize and struggle with moving forward. The subconscious sabotages you by prompting you to question everything, doubt yourself and many times paralyzes you so you don't do anything at all - holding you hostage, stuck in the mire of fear.

Know your subconscious isn't trying to punish you, it is trying to "protect" you, but when you take your power back, you also gain the power, wisdom and access to support to overcome limited, self sabotaging thinking and beliefs of the subconscious.

3. *Be WILLING* to rewrite your "subconscious records" (neural pathways of belief) - in essence be willing to do the inner work to align your conscious, subconscious and superconscious to create the highest outcome possible in every area of your life - *and... it is not as hard as you think!*

Your superconscious understands and knows without doubt that whatever you wish to experience is in your Field of Potentiality. What you want to be, do or have already exists at a higher plane of existence - it has your name on it.

When you consciously choose what you want, your subconscious will let you know if you're out of alignment with it by creating a feeling of resistance in your body. This is where so many people stop - because they believe the resistance energy is too painful or they don't know what to do with it - or both! Florence's simple teachings and the experiential Action Steps will show you what to do, but it is up to you to be willing to implement what you learn.

Remember, your subconscious runs the show and dictates your life experiences unless you consciously choose what you want - and it creates from thought patterns and beliefs that are limited, harsh and many times completely untrue!

RE: What does it mean when the
"Superconscious and Conscious out of alignment with the subconscious?"
This is when the subconscious does not believe you can have what you want
at a deep inner level due to a learned belief that is not true.
You probably are not even aware of this belief.
This belief is what is revealed for you to heal when you shift your energy to a higher vibration.

4. *Be WILLING* to allow yourself to dream Outrageously BIG without restraint!

You are a Master Creator! The only thing that holds you back is your own subconscious limited thoughts and beliefs. When you allow yourself to dream Outrageously BIG, you begin shifting your energy to Love or Above and the manifestation of prosperity is a direct result.

5. *Be WILLING* to choose to BE happy - no matter what your life looks like in this moment. And *BE WILLING* to claim your happiness without apology and follow through with making your interior energy of happiness your highest priority.

When your interior energy is of the happy Love or Above vibration consistently your external experiences mirror that Love or Above energy in miraculous ways.

You have the power to choose the existence you experience as your reality. Choosing to BE happy is NOT faking it till you make it. Choosing to be happy and shifting your energy into what happiness feels like for you as best you can; sets the wheels in motion to ***powerfully transform your life!***

6. *Be WILLING* to expand into the greatest, most magnificent expression of yourself - fully empowered - living from a deep source of love. *Aaahhhh.... feels good!*

7. *Be WILLING* to take the Action Steps necessary to manifest the life that brings you joy to experience - *your version of Heaven on Earth.*

Commitment

Make these commitments to yourself. Write them in the space provided under each one. Writing them down powerfully anchors the energy and sets into motion a shift in energy to create the highest possible outcome as your reality. If you feel resistance energy in your body, boldly clam and write out the statement anyway and begin now to transmute that lower vibration of fear energy to the higher vibration of love.

I, _____,

I am willing to release the need within me to worry and struggle.

_____

 I am willing to accept my life as it is.

_____

I am willing to release my fear of the unknown.

_____

I am willing to do the inner work when necessary to rewrite neural pathways of limiting beliefs to easily manifest what I want.

_____

_____

I am willing to dream outrageously big and embrace and live the excited, expectant, joy filled energy of living my dreams.

_____

_____

I choose to be happy and am willing to BE happy!

_____

I am willing to expand into and BE the greatest, most magnificent expression of myself!

_____

I am willing to take the necessary Action Steps to manifest my joy filled life - my version of Heaven on Earth!

_____

_____

Sign: _____

Date: _____

Manifesting What You Want is Simple

Choose to BE Happy.
Fearlessly *DECIDE* what you want and shift your energy to the Celebration of receiving.
Transform resistant fear energy to "Love or Above."
Demand and execute Action Steps.
Prepare to Receive.

Choose to BE Happy

Your thoughts and words are a vibration of energy. *"Change your expectancies (thoughts) and you change your conditions."* (Lecture: *What Do You Expect?*)

Your spiritual essence is housed in a human body - a body that is affected by the less than love fear, worry energy of our planet. As a human you experience life events that hurt you and leave you feeling like a victim.

However... once you get over the shock of a painful and/or traumatic life event, you have the ability to choose different thought vibrations. These life events are not what's causing your struggle, pain, discomfort, misery, unhappiness and stress. What is causing your struggle is your conscious or subconscious choice to hang on to the fear filled vibration of the initial experience. It's the energy of your thoughts and beliefs about your situation that not only cause you to suffer and struggle, but create more suffering and struggle as your continued experience

When you choose to experience a different reality of a higher vibration, you step out of the victim mentality of your circumstances and move into a state of acceptance. This doesn't mean that you're in agreement of your circumstances, and it doesn't mean you're "faking it till you make it," instead you're setting the foundation for the energetic shift to create something better - a higher outcome.

Set your intention and *"CHOOSE"* to be happy
no matter what your life looks like in this moment.

When you choose to be happy, you begin an energetic shift in your vibration of BE-ing that expands to align with your higher conscious state - your superconscious.

Note: Your superconscious knows without doubt that everything you want - Every - Thing - already exists at a higher plane of existence - it already has your name on it.

When you shift your energy within to a higher vibration - and maintain that vibration as much as humanly possible, the energy of your daily life experiences change, too.

Opportunities you didn't see before are revealed. Hope is restored and you become aware of the limitless possibilities on your life path. And... you attract to you through your higher vibrating energy of happiness the experience of a higher outcome - quite possibly better than you could have imagined.

Plus... when you choose to BE Happy, you choose your energy from this moment. Allow yourself to accept that it is in this moment of NOW that you are most powerful! In this moment, there is no past, there is no future, there is only now - and in this moment of now, you have the power to BE whatever expression of energy you wish.

Contemplate this: If you close your eyes right now and think about what you would really like to experience, your human brain doesn't know if you're really experiencing it or if you are simply thinking about it. Some people would call this daydreaming. The reality is, this is visioning - this is perpetuating the energy of manifesting something new and exciting!

When you employ all your senses in this visioning process, you are powerfully molding Raw Creation Energy into form.

You have the power to choose "love or above" energy of joy or "less than love" energy of suffering, worrying and despair.

Choose Love or Above and BE Happy!

Fearlessly DECIDE what you want and shift your energy to the Celebration of receiving.

Allow yourself to dream big - Outrageously BIG! Decide what you want to be, do or have as your experience and powerfully set your intention energetically.

Your superconscious or higher self, knows that whatever you wish to experience in your human life is already yours at a higher plane of existence. Clearly defining what you want brings your conscious and superconscious into alignment.

Make. The. Conscious. Decision!

When you decide on what you want, the spark of your thoughts begin to form matter - creation energy - into what you wish to experience. The energy of your decisive thoughts propel your life and build the momentum for you to *"breathe and live into"* the realization of your decision.

Maintaining that energy as much as humanly possible makes receiving what you want ==>inevitable<==

When you fearlessly decide what you want, focus on and celebrate the joy that receiving what you want will give you, the joy of receipt shifts your energy to the higher vibration of love.

BE nonresistant - unattached - to the outcome. This means release the need to worry about whether you'll receive it or not. The only reason humans are "attached" to an outcome is because at some level, maybe subconsciously, we are afraid we won't get what we want.

Being unattached to an outcome does not mean don't be excited about receiving it. On the contrary, it is vitally important to shift your energy from the energy of "I don't have what I want" to BE the excited expectant, joy filled energy of receiving! Manifesting what you want hinges on your energy of the joy receiving what you want will bring you! BE joyful! Celebrate receipt of what you want when there's no sign of in sight!

Fearlessly - Expect - to - Manifest - what - you - want!

Maintaining this joy filled energy as much as humanly possible influences the manifestation of what you want to materialize in your 3D life. The vibration of this joy molds formless matter into tangible material things and experiences, opens the way for enlightenment and has the capacity to heal the physical body.

Transform resistant fear energy to "Love or Above."

When you choose to shift your energy to a higher vibration, the shift challenges your subconscious beliefs (neural pathways of belief) - knocking your subconscious and conscious out of alignment..

Your subconscious will let you know it is out of alignment with your conscious by creating an uncomfortable feeling of resistance in your body - you cannot mistake it - this feeling is very clear. You've probably ignored it in the past and it has become a "normal" part of your every day existence. But Florence's teachings will pull the darkness of resistance into the spotlight and the darkness cannot exist in the light.

When this resistance occurs it's a Golden Opportunity for you to follow the breadcrumbs of uncomfortable resistant energy to its core and re-write the subconscious belief (neural pathway) to what your conscious and superconscious know to be true: *You deserve to be, do or have whatever it is you wish to experience.*

Question is, what tool do you use? For a list of suggested tools, go to the chapter Transformation Tools at the back of the book. (If you are a GAME of LIFE Mastery Program student, use the tools in the Dynamic Mastery Tool Library.)

DON'T - GIVE - UP!

FEELING the uncomfortable resistance energy is the hardest part! The exercises in this workbook will guide you to follow the path of the uncomfortable energy to face, disconnect from and heal the energy at the core level.

Demand and execute Action Steps.

From the excited, joy filled energy of having already received what you want, Demand Manifestation.

Demand guidance to action steps (if there are any) to manifest what you want into your realm of experience. Listen to the intuition or nudging of your heart. Be open to a hunch and follow it.

But know that the #1 Action Step is to *Maintain* - *as-much-as-Humanly-Possible* your joy energy that receiving what you want will bring you!

Prepare to Receive.

Prepare to experience what you want and open your arms wide to receive - and celebrate receiving! No matter what you wish to manifest, you can prepare with tangible material things or experiences to receive.

Example: you want to manifest new furniture, but you don't have the money to purchase new furniture. Window shop, pick out what you want, make plans on what to do with your old furniture, clean the space for the new furniture, move other furniture around to provide space for the new furniture. Close your eyes and envision bringing the furniture home and experience the joy that having it will bring you.

This preparation process can be experienced with Every Thing you want - e.g. a new job, financial flow, relationships, material things, dropping weight --- EVERY THING!

When these steps are put into practice, receiving what you want becomes *inevitable.*

This process is NOT hard, it is actually fun and with just a little practice this process becomes your new "Normal" way of living your life.

Decide - Shift Energy - Manifest

It is this simple.

Powerful, Magical Affirmations by Florence

I have the magic purse of spirit. It can never be depleted. As money goes out, immediately money comes in, under grace in perfect ways.

I expect the unexpected, my glorious good now comes to pass, under grace in miraculous ways.

The genius within me is released. I now fulfill my destiny.

God makes a way where there is no way! I receive prosperity easily, under grace in miraculous ways.

The unexpected happens, my seemingly impossible good now comes to pass.

What God has done for others, He/She now does for me and more!

I stand on miracle ground. I now expand quickly into the divine plan of my life, where all conditions are permanently perfect.

The Lord is my shepherd, I shall never want.

I look with wonder at that which is before me and open my arms wide to graciously receive.

The long arm of God reaches out over people and conditions, controlling this situation and protecting my interests.

Now is the appointed time. Today is the day of my amazing good fortune.

My supply comes from God, and big happy financial surprises now come to me, under grace, in perfect ways.

SECTION I - Foundation for Success

The following lectures: *The Way of Abundance* and *Five of Them Were Wise*, set your foundation to powerfully shift your energy to create a higher outcome in all areas of your life. In her no-nonsense way, Florence very simply delivers insight into typical human beliefs and behaviors that limit us and opens the way for a new empowered perspective and understanding.

From this new perception of understanding you will develop a new ascended energetic way of thinking that establishes your new foundation for success.

You will stop the cycle of creating the same thing over and over again by now having the "eyes to see" opportunities to solve your old problems. From this new, exciting energy, you will create something new and different - something wonderful in all areas of your square of life: health, wealth, love and perfect self-expression.

Action Step 1 - Florence's Teachings Speak to Me Powerfully

Read through the chapters of Florence's lectures in this section and highlight what speaks to you. After the chapter, use the NOTES page to write about why the highlighted sections resonated with you. Explore through writing what was revealed to you about your thought patterns and beliefs. Make note of the energy of hope and possibility you feel in your body and embrace that energy.

Important Action Step: Write about what spoke to you the most and how it is relevant to your life today. As you write you will discover the resonating energy expands to energetic ascension. The energetic shift to the higher vibration of love opens the way for clarity of thinking and creative inspiration. Plus the ability to make decisions of your highest good becomes a spontaneous event.

Note: When you read Florence's teachings, your internal vibration of energy will ascend. With this ascension, resistance energy (your subconscious not being in agreement with your now conscious, aware state) will be revealed. Be sure to address any resistance energy that is revealed to you by using your tools. (If you are a student of the GAME of LIFE Mastery Program, be sure to access the Dynamic Mastery Tool Library.)

Action Step 2 - Daily Success Ritual

Humans excel when they implement rituals into their daily routine.

When you consciously choose the energy you wish to BE and experience, you take your power back from your subconscious running your life.

Create and establish your Daily Success Ritual and BE "Miracle Conscious" daily. Implementing a new personal routine will guarantee expanding into the greatest expression of yourself. In addition, when you practice this daily upon waking, the process becomes you new "normal" way of living. A brilliant side affect of this New Normal way of living is this: shifting and maintain your energy to a higher level consistently on a daily basis rewrites your neural pathways of belief from less than love to love or above!

Use the space to design your simple, fun ritual and implement it your daily routine to "wind yourself up" to manifest prosperity. This ritual can be as long or as short as you wish. Make it fun and exciting!

You may experience some trial and error in getting your "wind up" process just right: fun, easy to remember and easy to do.

Don't skip over this exercise. It's important! When you implement your success ritual as a daily routine, you will naturally, effortlessly, "live" into your manifesting energy B E-ing a consistent experience - which makes the manifestation of what you want inevitable!

Example:

* Decide on the energy of happiness that you wish to experience and shift into "expecting" it as the reality of your day - and ultimately your new life.
* Listen to music that charges your energy
* Meditate into joy
* Dance and/or Practice Yoga - stretching into your new Joy of BE-ing
* Send love and light, sincerely from you heart, to all aspects of your coming day to ensure the highest outcome possible
* Choose a powerful affirmation for your day; examples are listed on the Powerful, Magical Affirmations by Florence page and write your own.

NOTE: Sending love and light to a life experience or relationship is NOT the same as surrounding someone or something with love and light. To surround someone or something with love and light, all you need to do is set the intention. To send someone or something love and light, you must shift your energy from less than love TO love in order to send it. You cannot be in love and less than love energy at the same time. So the experience of sending love sincerely from your heart, shifts your energy, thereby ascending the outcome of your experiences.

Intention and Attention

Consciously setting your daily intention through your energy, then focusing your attention on that energy as you flow through your day creates your experience - and IS-Magical!

Set your intention for the energy of the day you desire to experience. You may not know what it looks like, but you can identify what you want it to *FEEL like.*

Then focus - your - attention on the energy of that experience, remaining open to intuitive guidance of action steps to take to achieve the energetic flow.

If you experience a hiccup, step back, breathe deeply and employ your Daily Success Ritual skills to recapture that joy filled anticipation energy of excitement. You have the power to course correct when your day goes awry.

Remember: YOU are the Master Creator of your life - set your intention, the focus your attention and you become an irresistible magnet for what you wish to experience!

Repeat the energy of your ritual often throughout your day to maintain your Miracle Consciousness.

Daily Success Ritual:

_____

_____

_____

_____

_____

_____

_____

_____

_____

_____

_____

_____

_____

_____

_____

_____

_____

_____

_____

_____

_____

_____

_____

_____

_____

Do not be discouraged if you find yourself tweaking your Daily Success Ritual. As you grow and expand, what works best for you will also grow and expand. Your Daily Success Ritual is a living breathing, fluid experience. It is not a square peg fitting into a square hole.

Action Step 3 - Manifesting Blueprint Form

To print duplicate Manifesting Blueprint Forms, go to the website: www.SoulKisses.com/success

Part 1 - Choose to be Happy

Open your heart to the limitless possibility that you are and DREAM Big - Outrageously BIG!

Write down what your ***biggest, happiest, most magnificent life*** feels like and looks like! If you cannot "see" it, do not worry - you can definitely *"FEEL"* what you want your life to BE when you apply yourself. Explore what makes your heart sing with joy and write about it here. Allow yourself to be as a child with no limits with full, excited, expectant energy of the very real opportunity to live this Happy Life!

My Biggest, Happiest, Most Magnificent Life:

_____

_____

_____

_____

_____

_____

_____

_____

_____

_____

_____

_____

_____

_____

_____

_____

_____

_____

_____

_____

_____

_____

_____

_____

_____

_____

_____

_____

_____

_____

_____

_____

_____

_____

_____

_____

_____

_____

_____

_____

_____

_____

_____

_____

_____

_____

_____

_____

_____

_____

_____

_____

Part 2 - Fearlessly decide what you want and Celebrate experiencing it

Decide on one thing you want to manifest. It can be a new experience, something material or a relationship.

Write in detail what you want to experience. If you want a new job, or a new house or a new car or a new relationship, you do NOT need to know what they will "look" like, but you MUST know what they will *"feel" like*. Be sure to include "this or better."

Declare what you want as an affirmation. An affirmation is an energy container of words that is supported by the energy of your beliefs. It is a declaration of what you wish to experience written in a context that is positive - as if it has already happened.

Also include (reword, if you wish, to be the most powerful for you): *"This experience is mine by divine right, under grace in a miraculous way - for the highest good of all - thank you, thank you, thank you."* Dr. Anne Marie Evers tells us "for the highest good of all" is the Safety Clause!

While writing, shift into the energy of what it will feel like to be, do or have what you want and joyfully celebrate the experience. Shift till you feel a FULL - Body - YES energy within you!

My Powerful Affirmation Container of Manifesting Energy:

_____

_____

_____

_____

_____

_____

_____

_____

_____

_____

_____

_____

_____

_____

_____

_____

_____

Part 3 - Transform resistant fear energy to Love or Above

This is the part of the Manifesting Blueprint that you will customize to your personal needs.

Resistance energy may not develop in your body - in which case, go to Part 3!

However, if you feel resistance energy in your body, identify where you feel it, and ask your angels to "show you" where the uncomfortable energy stems from.

The angels may show you an image or vision in your mind's eye, or you may hear a message of the source of your resistance, or you may simply experience a knowing within your heart.

Write whatever comes to you -- and if you feel you're not getting anything, not to worry -- the information you're looking for will come to you when you're taking a bath or shower, doing dishes, ortaking a walk. I call these moments "Distracted Concentration" - the time you're focused, yet in a relaxed way and the angels can get the message through your mind chatter.

Sometimes simply facing this energy is enough to dissipate it. You will know if the resistance dissipates because you'll feel lighter and the area where you felt the energy will feel excited about what you want to experience - instead of resistant.

If you need further assistance to transform this energy, use a Transformation Tool from the back of the book or one of your own to shift into and maintain Love or Above energy.

Write about this experience here:

Angels, show me where this resistance energy stems from: _____

_____

_____

_____

_____

_____

_____

_____

_____

_____

_____

_____

_____

_____

_____

_____

_____

_____

Transformation Tool(s) I used to dissolve the resistance energy and what I experienced: _____

_____

_____

_____

_____

_____

_____

_____

_____

_____

_____

_____

_____

_____

_____

My most powerful Transformation Tools are: _____

_____

_____

_____

_____

_____

_____

_____

_____

_____

_____

_____

_____

_____

_____

_____

_____

_____

_____

Part 4 - Demand and execute Action Steps

Demand Action Steps if there are any, other than maintaining the lover or above energy, to bring to fruition what you wish to experience and be open to the guidance. You may receive this guidance from within and/or from without as a hunch or intuition.

Action Steps I executed to manifest what I want:

Action Step 1: Maintain the excited energy of receipt - celebrate!

_____

_____

_____

_____

_____

_____

_____

_____

_____

_____

_____

_____

_____

_____

_____

_____

_____

_____

_____

_____

_____

_____

_____

_____

_____

_____

_____

_____

Part 5 - Prepare to receive.

Prepare to receive what you wish to be, do or have *when there is no sign of it in sight* and experience the CELEBRATION energy of receiving it as much as humanly possible.

Write down what you are doing to prepare and celebrate. Action Steps and Preparing are similar, but not the same, they engage different perspectives of your energetic flow to fully support you to maintain your manifesting momentum.

Examples: If you've demanded money, prepare to pay for whatever you want the money for. DO not prepare what you will say if you don't receive the money!

If you've demanded a new home, get a new welcome mat, or change of address forms.

If you've demanded a new job, select what you'll wear on your first day - and celebrate the new job - when there is no job in sight!

Preparation actions:

_____

_____

_____

_____

_____

_____

_____

_____

_____

_____

_____

_____

_____

_____

_____

_____

_____

_____

_____

_____

The Way of Abundance

"Then shalt thou lay up gold as dust " - Job 22:24

The way of abundance is a one-way street.

As the old saying is, "there are no two ways about it."

You are either heading for lack, or heading for abundance. The man with a rich consciousness and the man with a poor consciousness are not walking on the same mental street.

There is a lavish supply, divinely planned for each individual.

The rich man is tapping it, for rich thoughts produce rich surroundings.

Change your thoughts, and in the twinkling of an eye, all your conditions change. Your world is a world of crystallized ideas, crystallized words.

Sooner or later, you reap the fruits of your words and thoughts.

"Words are bodies or forces which move spirally and return in due season to cross the lives of their creators." People who are always talking lack and limitation, reap lack and limitation.

You cannot enter the Kingdom of Abundance bemoaning your lot.

I know a woman who had always been limited in her ideas of prosperity. She was continually making her old clothes "do," instead of buying new clothes. She was very careful of what money she had, and was always advising her husband not to spend so much. She said repeatedly, "I don't want anything I can't afford."

She couldn't afford much, so she didn't have much. Suddenly her whole world cracked up. Her husband left her, weary of her nagging and limited thoughts. She was in despair, when one day she came across a book on metaphysics. It explained the power of thought and words.

She realized that she had invited every unhappy experience by wrong thinking. She laughed heartily at her mistakes, and decided to profit by them. She determined *to prove the law of abundance*.

She used what money she had, fearlessly, to show her faith in her invisible supply. She relied upon God as the source of her prosperity. She no longer voiced lack and limitation. She kept herself feeling and looking prosperous.

Her old friends scarcely recognized her. She had swung into the way of abundance. More money came to her than she had ever had before. Unheard-of doors opened - amazing channels were freed. She became very successful in a work she had had no training for.

She found herself on *miracle ground*. What had happened?

She had changed the quality of her words and thoughts. She had taken God into her confidence, and into all her affairs. She had many eleventh hour demonstrations, but her supply always came, for she dug her ditches and gave thanks without wavering.

Someone called me up recently and said, "I am looking desperately for a position."

I replied, "Don't look desperately for it, look for it with praise and thanksgiving, for Jesus Christ, the greatest of metaphysicians, said to pray with praise and thanksgiving."

Praise and thanksgiving open the gates, for expectancy always wins.

Of course, the law is impersonal, and a dishonest person with rich thoughts will attract riches - but, "a thing ill-got has ever bad success," as Shakespeare says. It will be of short duration and will not bring happiness.

We have only to read the papers to see that the way of the transgressor is hard.

That is the reason it is so necessary to make your demands aright on the Universal Supply, and ask for what is yours by divine right and under grace in a perfect way.

Some people attract prosperity, but cannot hold it. Sometimes their heads are turned, sometimes they lose it through fear and worry.

A friend in one of my question and answer classes told this story.

Some people in his home town, who had always been poor, suddenly struck oil in their back yard. It brought great riches. The father joined the country club and went in for golf. He was no longer young - the exercise was too much for him and he dropped dead on the links.

This filled the whole family with fear. They all decided they might have heart trouble, so they are now in bed with trained nurses watching every heart beat.

In the race-thought people must worry about something.

They no longer worried about money, so they shifted their worries to health.

The old idea was, "that you can't have everything." If you got one thing, you'd lose another. People were always saying, "Your luck won't last," "It's too good to be true."

Jesus Christ said, "In the world (world thought) there is tribulation, but be of good cheer, I have overcome the world (thought)."

In the superconscious, there is a lavish supply for every demand, and your good is perfect and permanent.

"If thou return to the Almighty, thou shalt be built up (in consciousness), thou shalt put away iniquity far from thy tabernacles."

"Then shalt thou lay up gold as dust, the gold of Ophir as the stones of the brooks."

"Yea, the Almighty shall be thy defense and thou shalt have plenty of silver."

What a picture of opulence! The result of "Returning to the Almighty (in consciousness)."

With the average person (who has thought in terms of lack for a long time) it is very difficult to build up a rich consciousness.

I have a student who has attracted great success by making the statement: *"I am the daughter of the King! My rich Father now pours out his abundance upon me. I am the daughter of the King! Everything makes way for me."*

Many people put up with limited conditions because they are too lazy (mentally), to think themselves out of them.

You must have a great desire for financial freedom, you must feel yourself rich, you must see yourself rich, you must continually prepare for riches. Become as a little child and make believe you are rich. You are then impressing the subconscious with expectancy.

The imagination is man's workshop, the scissors of the mind, where he is constantly cutting out the events of his life!

The superconscious is the realm of inspiration, revelation, illumination and intuition.

Intuition is usually known as a hunch. I do not apologize for the word "hunch" anymore. It is now in Webster's latest dictionary.

I had a hunch to look up "hunch," and there it was.

The superconscious is the realm of perfect ideas. The great genius captures his thoughts from the superconscious.

"Without the vision (imagination) my people perish."

When people have lost the power to image their good, they "perish" (or go under).

It is interesting to compare the translation of the French and English Bibles. In the 21st verse of the 22nd chapter of Job we read: "Acquaint now thyself with him, and be at peace, thereby good shall come unto thee." In the French Bible we read: "Attach thyself to God and you will have peace. Thou shalt thus enjoy happiness."

The 23rd verse: "If thou return to the Almighty, thou shalt be built up, thou shalt put away iniquity far from thy tabernacles." In the French translation we read "Thou shalt be re-established if thou returnest to the Almighty, putting iniquity far off from your dwellings."

In the 24th verse we read a new and amazing translation. The English Bible reads, "Then shalt thou lay up gold as dust, and the gold of Ophir as the stones of the brooks." The French Bible says: "Throw gold into the dust, the gold of Ophir amongst the pebbles of the torrents, and the Almighty shall be thy gold, thy silver, thy riches."

This means if people are depending entirely on their visible supply, it is even better to throw it away and trust absolutely to the Almighty for gold, silver and riches.

I give an example in the story told me by a friend.

A priest went to visit a nunnery in France, where they fed many children. One of the nuns, in despair, told the priest they had no food, the children must go hungry. She said that they had but one piece of silver (about the value of a quarter of a dollar). They needed food and clothing.

The priest said, "Give me the coin."

She handed it to him and he threw it out the window.

"Now," he said, "rely entirely upon God."

Within a short time friends arrived with plenty of food and gifts of money.

This doesn't mean to throw away what money you have, but don't depend upon it. *Depend upon your invisible supply, the Bank of the Imagination.*

Let us now attach ourselves to God and have peace. For He shall be our gold, our silver and our riches.

The inspiration of the Almighty shall be my defense and I shall have plenty of silver.

NOTES

And Five of Them Were Wise

"And five of them were wise, and five were foolish.
They that were foolish took their lamps, and took no oil with them." - Matthew 25:2-3

My subject is the parable of the Wise and Foolish Virgins. "And five of them were wise, and five were foolish. They that were foolish took their lamps, and took no oil with them. But the wise took oil in their vessels with their lamps." The parable teaches that true prayer means preparation.

Jesus Christ said, "And all things, whatsoever ye shall ask in prayer, *believing,* ye shall receive" (Math. 21:22). "Therefore I say unto you, what things soever ye desire, when ye pray, believe that ye receive them, and ye shall have them" (Mark 11:24). In this parable he shows that only those who have prepared for their good (thereby showing active faith) will bring the manifestation to pass.

We might paraphrase the scriptures and say: When ye pray believe ye have it. When ye pray ACT as if you have already received.

Armchair faith or rocking chair faith, will never move mountains. In the armchair, in the silence, or meditation, you are filled with the wonder of this Truth, and feel that your faith will never waver. You know that The Lord is your Shepherd, you shall never want.

You feel that your God of Plenty will wipe out all burdens of debt or limitations. Then you leave your armchair and step out into the arena of Life. It is only what you do in the arena that counts.

I will you give you an illustration showing how the law works; for faith without action is dead.

A man, one of my students, had a great desire to go abroad. He took the statement: *I give thanks for my divinely designed trip, divinely financed, under grace, in a perfect way.* He had very little money, but knowing the law of preparation, he bought a trunk. It was a very gay and happy trunk with a big red band around its waist. Whenever he looked at it it gave him a realization of a trip. One day he seemed to feel his room moving. He felt the motion of a ship. He went to the window to breathe the fresh air, and it smelt like the aroma of the docks. With his inner ear he heard the shriek of a sea-gull and the creaking of the gangplank. The trunk had commenced to work. It had put him in the vibration of his trip. Soon after that, a large sum of money came to him and he took the trip. He said afterwards that it was perfect in every detail.

In the arena of Life we must keep ourselves tuned-up to concert pitch.

Are we acting from motives of fear or faith? *Watch your motives with all diligence, for out of them are the issues of life.*

If your problem is a financial one (and it usually is) you must know how to wind yourself up financially, and keep wound up by always acting your faith. The material attitude towards money is to trust in your salary, your income and investments, which can shrink over night.

The spiritual attitude toward money is to trust in God for your supply. To keep your possessions, always realize that they are God in manifestation. "What Allah has given cannot be diminished," then if one door shuts another door, immediately opens.

Never voice lack or limitation for "by your words you are condemned." You combine with what you notice, and if you are always noticing failure and hard times, you will combine with failure and hard times.

You must form the habit of living in the fourth dimension, "The World of the Wondrous." It is the world where you do not judge by appearances.

You have trained your inner eye to see through failure into success, to see through sickness into health to see through limitation into plenty. "I will give you the land which you thou seeth."

The man who achieves success has the *fixed idea of success.* If it is founded on a rock of truth and rightness it will stand. If not, it is built upon sand and washed into the sea, returning to its native nothingness.

Only divine ideas can endure. Evil destroys itself, for it is a cross current against universal order, and the way of the transgressor is hard.

"They that were foolish took their lamps, and took no oil with them. But the wise took oil in their vessels with their lamps."

The lamp symbolizes man's consciousness. The oil is what brings Light or understanding.

"While the bridegroom tarried, they all slumbered and slept. And at midnight there was a cry made. Behold, the bridegroom cometh; go ye out to meet him. Then all those virgins arose, and trimmed their lamps. And the foolish said unto the wise, Give us your oil; for our lamps are gone out."

The foolish virgins were without wisdom or understanding, which is oil for the consciousness, and when they were confronted with a serious situation, they had no way of handling it.

And when they said to the wise "give us of your oil," the wise answered saying, "Not so; lest there be not enough for us and you: but go ye rather to them that sell, and buy for yourselves."

That means that the foolish virgins could *not receive more than was in their consciousness,* or what they were vibrating to.

The man received the trip because it was in his consciousness, as a reality. He believed that he had already received. As he prepared for the trip he was taking oil for his lamps. With *realization comes manifestation.*

The law of preparation works both ways. If you prepare for what you fear or don't want, you begin to attract it. David said, "The thing I feared has come upon me." We hear people say, "I must put away money in case of illness." They are deliberately preparing to be ill. Or, "I'm saving for a rainy day." The rainy day is sure to come, at a most inconvenient time.

The divine idea for every man is plenty. Your barns should be full, and your cup should flow over, but we must learn to ask aright.

For example take this statement: *I call on the law of accumulation. My supply comes from God, and now pours in and piles up, under grace.*

This statement does not give any picture of stint or saving or sickness. It gives a fourth dimensional feeling of abundance, leaving the channels to Infinite Intelligence.

Every day you must make a choice, will you be wise or foolish? Will you prepare for your good? Will you *take the giant swing into faith?* Or serve doubt and fear and bring no oil for your lamps?

"And while they went to buy, the bridegroom came; and they that were ready went in with him to the marriage: and the door was shut. Afterward came also the other virgins, saying, Lord, Lord, open to us. But he answered and said, Verily I say unto you, I know you not."

You may feel that the foolish virgins paid very dearly for neglecting to bring oil for their lamps, but we are dealing with the law of Karma (or the law of come back). It has been called the "judgment day," which people usually associate with the end of the world.

Your judgment day comes, they say, in sevens - seven hours, seven days, seven weeks, seven months, or seven years. It might even come in seven minutes. Then you pay some Karmic debt; the price for having violated spiritual law. *You failed to trust God, you took no oil for your lamps.*

Every day examine your consciousness and see just what your are preparing for. You are fearful of lack and hang on to every cent, thereby attracting more lack. Use what you have with wisdom and it opens the way for more to come to you.

In my book, "Your Word Is Your Wand," I tell about the Magic Purse. In the Arabian Nights they tell the story of a man who had a Magic Purse. As money went out, immediately money appeared in it again.

So I made the Statement: *My supply comes from God - I have the magic purse of the spirit. It can never be depleted. As money goes out, immediately money comes in. It is always crammed, jammed with abundance, under grace, in perfect ways.*

This brings a vivid picture to mind: You are drawing on the bank of the imagination.

A woman who did not have much money was afraid to pay any bills and see her bank account dwindle. It came to her with great conviction: *"I have the magic purse of the spirit. It can never be depleted. As money goes out, immediately, money comes in."* She fearlessly paid her bills, and several large cheques came to her that she did not expect.

"Watch and pray lest ye enter into the temptation" of preparing for something destructive instead of something constructive.

I knew a woman who told me she always kept a long crepe veil handy in case of funerals. I said to her, "You are a menace to your relatives, and are preparing to hurry them all off, so that you can wear the veil." She destroyed it.

Another woman who had no money decided to send her two daughters to college. Her husband scorned the idea and said, "Who will pay their tuition? I have no money for it." She replied, *"I know some unforeseen good will come to us."* She kept on preparing her daughters for college. Her husband laughed heartily and told all their friends that his wife was sending the girls to college on "some unforeseen good." A rich relative suddenly sent her a large sum of money. "Some unforeseen good" *did* arrive, for she had shown active faith. I asked what she had said to her husband when the cheque arrived. She replied, "Oh, I never antagonize George by telling him I am in the right."

So prepare for your "unforeseen good." Let every thought and every act express your unwavering faith. Every event in your life is a crystallized idea. Something you have invited through either fear or faith. *Something you have prepared for.*

So let us be wise and bring oil for our lamps - and when we least expect it, we shall reap the fruits of our faith.

My lamps are now filled with the oil of faith and fulfillment.

NOTES

_____

_____

_____

_____

_____

_____

_____

_____

_____

_____

_____

_____

_____

_____

_____

_____

_____

_____

_____

_____

_____

_____

_____

_____

_____

_____

_____

_____

_____

_____

SECTION II - Expecting and Receiving Miracles

The following lectures, *What Do You Expect?*, *Rivers in the Desert*, and *Bricks without Straw*, hold the energy of support to open your heart to expect and receive miracles.

Florence was well known for providing "treatments" and "speaking the word" for her students. Both a treatment and speaking the word held unparalleled energy of support for the student. They were so powerful because Florence knew, *without any doubt*, that whatever her students wanted to experience was already theirs at a higher plane of existence. So it was easy for her to hold the energy with the student of already having received what they wanted to experience.

You are powerful in your own right. Powerful enough to hold the energy to manifest what you want. Having additional support, such as a friend, partner or teacher, to help you hold the energy empowers you exponentially. (Both the GAME of LIFE Mastery Program and the Secret Door to Success MASTERMIND include private Facebook communities of support - www.theGAMEofLIFEmastery.com and www.MySecretDoorToSuccess.com respectively.)

The next three lectures will further support you to open your heart to shift to a Miracle Consciousness - holding the energy to *Expect and Receive Miracles.*

As you read through each chapter, allow your spiritual BE-ingness to expand into a greater expression of yourself. This experience is an expansion of consciousness.

Be aware that when you expand your energy, you may experience a contraction of energy. Do not be alarmed if this happens. A contraction is normal and will support you by revealing the energy of a thought pattern or belief that no longer serves you.

This revelation is a golden opportunity to identify, defeat and conquer the resistance energy of something that is not true about yourself and rewrite your neural pathway of belief.

By rewriting your "subconscious record" as Florence calls it, to what is true about yourself, you will be free to create a new reality. You will experience a different, expanded mindset to create a higher outcome.

Action Step 1 - Florence's Teachings Speak to Me Powerfully

Read through the chapters of Florence's lectures in this section and highlight what speaks to you. After the chapter, use the NOTES page to write about why the highlighted sections resonated with you. Explore through writing what was revealed to you about your thought patterns and beliefs. Make note of the energy of hope and possibility you feel in your body and embrace that energy.

Important Action Step: Write about what spoke to you the most and how it is relevant to your life today.

Note: When you read Florence's teachings, your internal vibration of energy will ascend. With this ascension, resistance energy (your subconscious not being in agreement with your now conscious, aware state) will be revealed. Be sure to address any resistance energy that is revealed to you by using your tools. (If you are a student of the GAME of LIFE Mastery Program, be sure to access the Dynamic Mastery Tool Library.)

Action Step 2 - Transforming Resistance

You're expanding your consciousness and becoming the person who experiences what you wish to manifest. The more you define who you want to BE, the easier it will be to flow into BEing that person.

When you make the choice to experience a different reality, you bring into alignment your conscious and your superconscious. This shift of your energy to the higher vibration of love or above, may not be in alignment with your subconscious beliefs.

When your conscious is out of alignment with your subconscious, you will feel an uncomfortable energy of resistance in your body. This block or "King-Pin" of energy is what is between you and what you wish to experience.

The revelation of this energy is when most people "Give-Up" because they believe transforming their life is too painful.

A little known secret is this:

the energy of resistance that is revealed is as painful as it gets!
.....and you've already experienced it!

Look within and follow the breadcrumbs of the uncomfortable energy to its core and face it, disconnect from it and heal it. Ask your angels to "show you" the core of the energy. If you need additional help disconnecting from the cords of this energy, Kate has a "Disconnect the Cords to Heal the Wounds of Your Heart" program that is magical. You may learn more about this program at www.SoulKisses.com/success.

What resistant energy has come up for you? Again, do not give in to the human desire to quit and revert back to less than love energy as your normal way of living when resistance is revealed.

What healing did you experience as you fearlessly faced the energy with the assistance of your Angelic A-Team --- freedom? empowerment? Relief? Did you get a glimpse of the unconditional, powerful love that you are?

What tools did you use? Learning what tools work best for you to process through energy of thought patterns and beliefs that have held you back will make your life so-much-easier! *Be sure to include them in your customized personal Manifesting Blueprint.*

NOTE: Know that when you begin to shift your energy - and simply READING Florence's teachings will begin that shift - you set the energetic wheels in motion to transform your life to a higher outcome of experience. Keep Going!

After you read this section of lectures, return here and write about your experience facing resistance energy:

_____

_____

_____

_____

_____

_____

_____

_____

_____

_____

_____

_____

_____

_____

_____

_____

_____

_____

_____

_____

_____

_____

_____

_____

_____

_____

_____

_____

_____

_____

_____

RECAP

Are you settling into and perfecting your Daily Success Ritual?

Repetition expands the higher vibration of love exponentially when you take this Action Step daily and throughout your day. Monitoring your energetic vibration and maintaining it at Love or Above as much as humanly possible will rewrite your neural pathways of belief of being limited to *BE-ing Limitless - knowing from a deep soul level that Any-Thing is possible!*

You can do this!!

_____

_____

_____

_____

_____

_____

_____

_____

_____

_____

_____

_____

_____

_____

_____

_____

_____

_____

_____

_____

_____

_____

_____

What Do You Expect?

"According to your faith be it unto you." - Matthew 9:29

Faith is expectancy, "According to your faith, be it unto you."

We might say, according to your expectancies be it done unto you; so, what are you expecting?

We hear people say: "We expect the worst to happen," or "The worst is yet to come." They are deliberately inviting the worst to come.

We hear others say: "I expect a change for the better." They are inviting better conditions into their lives.

Change your expectancies and you change your conditions.

How can you change your expectancies, when you have formed the habit of expecting loss, lack or failure?

Begin to act as if you *expected* success, happiness and abundance; *prepare for your good.*

Do something to show you expect it to come. Active faith alone, will impress the subconscious.

If you have spoken the word for a home, prepare for it immediately, as if you hadn't a moment to lose. Collect little ornaments, table-cloths, etc., etc.!

I knew a woman who made the giant swing into faith, by buying a large arm-chair; a chair meant business, she bought a large and comfortable chair, for she was preparing for the right man. He came.

Someone will say, "Suppose you haven't money to buy ornaments or a chair?" Then look in shop windows and link with them in thought.

Get in their vibration: I sometimes hear people say; "I don't go into the shops because I can't afford to buy anything." That is just the reason why you should go into the shops. Begin to make friends with the things you desire or require.

I know a woman who wanted a ring. She went boldly to the ring department and tried on rings.

It gave her such a realization of ownership, that not long after, a friend made her a gift of a ring. "You combine with what you notice."

Keep on noticing beautiful things, and you make an invisible contact. Sooner or later these things are drawn into your life, unless you say, "Poor me, too good to be true."

"My soul, wait thou only upon God: for my expectation is from Him." This is a most important statement from the 62nd Psalm.

The soul is the subconscious mind, and the psalmist was telling his subconscious to expect everything directly from the universal; not to depend upon doors and channels; "My expectation is from Him."

God cannot fail, for "His ways are ingenious, His methods are sure."

You can expect any seemingly impossible Good from God; if you do not limit the channels.

Do not say how you want it done, or how it can't be done.

"God is the Giver and the Gift *and creates His own amazing channels.*"

Take the following statement: *I cannot be separated from God the Giver, therefore, I cannot be separated from God the Gift. The gift is God in action.*

Get the realization that every blessing is *Good in action,* and see God in every face and good in every situation. This makes you master of all conditions.

A woman came to me saying that there was no heat in the radiators in their apartment, and that her mother was suffering from the cold. She added, "The landlord has declared that we can't have heat until a certain date." I replied, "God is your landlord." She said, "That's all I want to know," and rushed out. That evening the heat was turned on without asking. It was because she realized that the landlord was God in manifestation.

This is a wonderful age, for people are becoming Miracle Minded; it is in the air.

Quoting from an article which I found in the New York Journal and American by John Anderson, it corroborates what I have just said.

The title of the article is "Theatre Goers Make Hits of Metaphysical Plays."

If, said the cynical manager, who shall be called Brock Pemberton, with a slight accent of sarcasm in his voice, the other night, on an intermission curbside talk, you fellows meaning the critics, know so much about what the New York public wants, why don't you tell me what to produce? Why don't you run me into business instead of out of it? "Why don't you tell me what sort of play the play-goers want to see?" "I would," I said, "But you wouldn't believe it."

"You're hedging," he said, "You don't know, and you're trying to cover up by pretending to know more than you're willing to say. You haven't any more idea than I have this minute what sort of plays generally succeed."

"I have," I said, "there is one sure fire success; one theme that works and has always worked, whether it is competing with boy meets girl, mysteries, historical tragedies, etc., no play on the theme has ever completely failed if it had any merit at all, and a lot of poor ones have been big hits."

"You're stalling again," said Mr. Pemberton, "What sort of plays are they?"

"Metaphysical," I said, fouling slightly with a big word and waiting quietly for the effect. "Metaphysical," said Mr. Pemberton, "You mean metaphysical?"

I paused a moment and since Mr. Pemberton said nothing, went right on spouting such titles as "The Green Pastures," "The Star Wagon," "Father Malachy's Miracle!, etc." "Some of these," I added, "reached the public over the heads of the critics." But Mr. Pemberton had departed to ask probably, in every theatre in town, "Is there a metaphysician in the house?"

People are beginning to realize the power of their words and thoughts. They understand *why* "Faith is the substance of the thing hoped for, the evidence of things not seen."

We see the law of expectancy working out through superstition.

If you walk under a ladder and expect it to give you bad luck, it will give you bad luck. The ladder is quite innocent; bad luck came because you expected it.

We might say, expectancy is the substance of the things hoped for, or expectancy is the substance of the thing man fears. "The thing I expected has come upon me."

Nothing is too good to be true, nothing is too wonderful to happen, nothing is too good to last, when you look to God for your good.

Now think of the blessings which seem so far off, and begin to expect them *now*, under grace, in an unexpected way; for God works in unexpected ways, His wonders to perform.

I was told that there are three thousand promises in the Bible.

Let us now expect all these blessings to come to pass. Among them we are promised Riches and Honor, Eternal Youth ("Your flesh shall become as a little child's") and Eternal Life, ("Death itself shall be overcome.")

Christianity is founded upon the forgiveness of sins and an empty tomb.

We now know that all these things are scientifically possible.

As we call on the law of forgiveness, we become free from mistakes and the consequences of mistakes, ("Though your sins be as scarlet ye shall be washed whiter than wool.")

Then our bodies will be bathed in Light, and express the "body electric," which is incorruptible and indestructible, pure substance, expressing perfection.

I expect the unexpected, my glorious good now comes to pass.

NOTES

_____

_____

_____

_____

_____

_____

_____

_____

_____

_____

_____

_____

_____

_____

_____

_____

_____

_____

_____

_____

_____

_____

_____

_____

_____

_____

_____

_____

_____

_____

_____

_____

Rivers in the Desert

*"Behold, I will do a new thing: now it shall spring forth; shall ye not know it?
I will even make a way in the wilderness, and rivers in the desert."* - Isaiah 43:19

In this 43rd chapter of Isaiah, are many wonderful statements, showing the irresistible power of Supreme Intelligence, coming to man's rescue in times of trouble. *No matter how impossible the situation seems, Infinite Intelligence knows the way out.*

Working with God - Power, man becomes unconditioned and absolute. Let us get a realization of this hidden power that we can call upon at any moment.

Make your contact with Infinite Intelligence, (the God within) and all appearance of evil evaporates, for it comes from man's "vain imaginings."

In my question and answer class I would be asked, "How do you make a conscious contact with this Invincible Power?"

I reply, "By your word." "By your word you are justified."

The Centurion said to Jesus Christ, "Speak the word master and my servant shall be healed."

"Whosoever calleth on the name of the Lord shall be delivered." Notice the word, "call" you are calling on the Lord or Law, when you make an affirmation of Truth.

As I always say, take a statement which "clicks," that means, gives you a feeling of security.

People are enslaved by ideas of lack; lack of love, lack of money, lack of companionship, lack of health, and so on.

They are enslaved by the ideas of interference and incompletion. They are asleep in the Adamic Dream: Adam (generic man) ate of "Maya the tree of illusion" and saw two powers, good and evil.

The Christ mission was to wake people up to the Truth of one power, God. "Awake thou that sleepeth."

If you lack any good thing, you are still asleep to your good.

How do you awake from the Adamic dream of opposites, after having slept soundly in the race thought for hundreds of years?

Jesus Christ said, "When two of you agree, it shall be done." It is the law of agreement.

It is almost impossible to see clearly, your good, for yourself: that is where the healer, practitioner or friend is necessary.

Many successful men say they have succeeded because their wives believed in them.

I will quote from a current newspaper, giving Walter P. Chrysler's tribute to his wife, "Nothing," he once said, "has given me more satisfaction in life, than the way my wife had faith in me from the very first, through all those years." Chrysler wrote of her, "It seemed to me I could not make anyone understand that I was ambitious except Della. I could tell her and she would nod. It seems to me I even dared to tell her that I intended, some day, to be a master mechanic." She always backed his ambitions.

Talk about your affairs as little as possible, and then only to the ones who will give you encouragement and inspiration. The world is full of "wet blankets," people who will tell you "it can't be done, that you are aiming too high."

As people sit in Truth meetings and services, often a word or an idea will open a way in the wilderness.

Of course the Bible is speaking of states of consciousness. You are in a wilderness or desert, when you are out of harmony ‑ when you are angry, resentful, fearful or undecided. Indecision is the cause of much ill health, being unable "to make up your mind."

One day when I was in a bus, a woman stopped it and asked the conductor its destination. He told her, but she was undecided. She got half way on, and then got off, then on again: the conductor turned to her and said, "Lady, make up your mind!"

So it is with so many people, "Ladies make up your minds!"

The intuitive person is never undecided, he is given his leads and hunches, and goes boldly ahead, knowing he is on the magic path.

In Truth, we always ask for definite leads just what to do; you will always receive one if you ask for it. Sometimes it comes as intuition, sometimes from the external.

One of my students, named Ada, was walking down the street, undecided whether to go to a certain place or not. She asked for a lead. Two women were walking in front of her. One turned to the other and said, "Why don't you go Ada?" The woman's name just happened to be Ada, my friend took it as a definite lead, and went on to her destination, and the outcome was very successful.

We really lead magic lives, guided and provided for at every step; *if we have ears to hear and eyes that see.*

Of course we have left the plane of the intellect and are drawing from the superconscious, the God within, which says, "This is the way, walk ye in it."

Whatever you should know, will be revealed to you. Whatever you lack, will be provided! "Thus saith the Lord which maketh a way in the sea and a path in the mighty waters."

"Remember ye not the former things, neither consider the things of old."

People who live in the past have severed their contact with the wonderful *now*. God knows only the now. Now is the appointed time, today is the day.

Many people lead lives of limitation, hoarding and saving, afraid to use what they have; which brings more lack and more limitation.

I give the example of a woman who lived in a small country town. She could scarcely see to get about, and had very little money. A kind friend took her to an oculist, and presented her with glasses, which enabled her to see perfectly. Sometime later she met her on the street without the glasses. She exclaimed, "Where are your glasses?"

The woman replied, "Well, you don't expect me to hack 'em out by using them every day, do you? I only wear them on Sundays."

You must live in the now and be wide awake to your opportunities.

"Behold, I will do a new thing, now it shall spring forth; shall ye not know it? I will even make a way in the wilderness, and rivers in the desert."

This message is meant for the individual. Think of your problem and know that Infinite Intelligence knows the way of fulfillment. I say the *way,* for before you called you were answered. *The supply always precedes the demand.*

God is the Giver and the Gift and now creates His own amazing channels.

When you have asked for the Divine Plan of your life to manifest, you are protected from getting the things that are not in the Divine Plan.

You may think that all your happiness depends upon obtaining one particular thing in life; later on, you praise the Lord that you didn't get it.

Sometimes you are tempted to follow the reasoning mind, and argue with your intuitive leads, suddenly the Hand of Destiny pushes you into your right place, and under grace, you find yourself back on the magic path again.

You are now wide awake to your good, you have the ears that hear (your intuitive leads), and the eyes which see the open road of fulfillment.

"The genius within me is released. I now fulfill my destiny."

NOTES

_____

_____

_____

_____

_____

_____

_____

_____

_____

_____

_____

_____

_____

_____

_____

_____

_____

_____

_____

_____

_____

_____

_____

_____

_____

_____

_____

_____

_____

_____

Bricks without Straw

"There shall no straw be given you, yet ye shall make bricks without straw." - Exodus 5:18

In the 5th chapter of Exodus, we have a picture of every day life, when giving a metaphysical interpretation.

The Children of Israel were in bondage to Pharaoh, the cruel taskmaster, ruler of Egypt. They were kept in slavery, making bricks, and were hated and despised.

Moses had orders from the Lord to deliver his people from bondage - "Moses and Aaron went in and told Pharaoh -- Thus saith the Lord God of Israel, Let my people go, that they may hold a feast unto me in the wilderness."

He not only refused to let them go, but told them he would make their tasks even more difficult: they must make bricks without straw being provided for them.

"And the task-masters of the people went out, and their officers, and they spake to the people, saying, Thus saith Pharaoh, I will not give you straw."

"Go ye, get you straw where ye can find it: yet not ought of your work shall be diminished."

It was impossible to make bricks without straw. The Children of Israel were completely crushed by Pharaoh, they were beaten for not producing the bricks -- Then came the message from Jehovah.

"Go therefore now, and work; for there shall no straw be given you, yet shall ye deliver the tale (number) of bricks."

Working with Spiritual law they could make bricks without straw, which means to accomplish the seemingly impossible.

How often in life people are confronted with this situation.

Agnes M. Lawson in her "Hints to Bible Students" says -- "The Life in Egypt under foreign oppression is the symbol of man under the hard taskmasters of Destructive thinking, Pride, Fear, Resentment, Ill-will, etc. The deliverance under Moses is the freedom man gains from the taskmasters, as he learns the law of life, for we can never come under grace, except we first know the law. The law must be made known in order to be fulfilled."

In the 111th Psalm we read in the final verse, "The fear of the Lord (law) is the beginning of Wisdom: a good understanding have all they that do his commandments: his praise endureth forever."

Now if we read the word Lord (law) it will give us the key to the statement.

The fear of the law (Karmic law) is the beginning of wisdom (not the fear of the Lord).

When we know that whatever we send out comes back, we begin to be afraid of our own boomerangs.

I read in a medical journal the following facts telling of the Boomerang this great Pharaoh received.

It would appear that flesh is indeed heir to a long and ancient line of ills, when, as was revealed by Lord Monyahan at a lecture at Leeds, that the Pharaoh of the oppression suffered from hardening of the heart in a literal sense. Lord Monyahan showed some remarkable photographic slides of results of surgical operations a thousand years before Christ, and among these was a slide of the actual anatomical remains of the Pharaoh of the Oppression.

"The large vessel springing from the heart was in such a well-preserved state, as to enable sections of it to be made recently from the lantern slide. It was impossible to distinguish between the ancient and modern vessel. Both hearts had been attacked by Atheroma, a condition in which calcium salts are deposited in the walls of the vessel, making it rigid and inelastic."

Inadequate expanse to the stream of blood from the heart caused the vessel to give way; with this condition went the mental changes that occur with a rigid arterial system: *A narrowness of outlook; restriction and dread of enterprise, a literal hardening of the heart.*

So Pharaoh's hardness of heart, hardened his own heart.

This is as true today as it was several thousand years ago -- we are all coming out of the Land of Egypt, out of the House of Bondage.

Your doubts and fears keep you in slavery; you face a situation which seems hopeless. What can you do? It is a case of making bricks without straw.

But remember the words of Jehovah, "Go therefore now, and work; for there shall no straw be given you, yet shall ye deliver the tale (number) of bricks."

You shall make bricks without straw. God makes a way where there is no way!

I was told the story of a woman who needed money for her rent. It was necessary to have it at once, but she knew of no channel, she exhausted every avenue.

However, she was a Truth student, and kept making her affirmations.

Her dog whined and wanted to go out, she put on his leash and walked down the street, in the accustomed direction.

However, the dog pulled at his leash and wanted to go in another direction.

She followed, and in the middle of the block, opposite an open park, she looked down, and picked up a roll of bills, which exactly covered rent.

She looked for ads, but never found the owner. There were no houses near where she found it.

The reasoning mind, the intellect, takes the throne of Pharaoh in your consciousness. It says continually, "It can't be done. What's the use!"

We must drown out these dreary suggestions with a vital affirmation!

For example take this statement: *"The unexpected happens, my seemingly impossible good now comes to pass."* This stops all argument from the army of the aliens (the reasoning mind.).

"The unexpected happens!" That is an idea it cannot cope with.

"Thou hast made me wiser than mine enemies." Your enemy thoughts, your doubts, fears and apprehensions!

Think of the joy of really being free forever, from the Pharaoh of the oppression. To have the idea of *security, health, happiness and abundance established in the subconscious.* It would mean a life free from all limitation!

It would be the Kingdom which Jesus Christ spoke of, where all things are automatically added unto us. I say automatically added unto us, because all life is vibration; and when we vibrate to success, happiness and abundance, the things which symbolize these states of consciousness will attach themselves to us.

Feel rich and successful, and suddenly you receive a large cheque or a beautiful gift.

I tell the story showing the working of this law. I went to a party where people played games, and whoever won, received a gift. The prize was a beautiful fan.

Among those present, was a very rich woman, who had everything. Her name was Clara. The poorer and resentful ones got together and whispered: "We hope Clara doesn't get the fan." Of course Clara won the fan.

She was care-free and vibrating to abundance. *Envy and resentment short-circuit your good* and keep away your fans.

If you should happen to be resentful and envious, take the statement: *What God has done for others He now does for me and more!*

Then all the fans and things will come your way.

No man gives to himself but himself, and no man takes away from himself but himself. The "Game of Life" is a game of solitaire; as you change, all conditions will change.

Now to go back to Pharaoh the oppressor; no one loves an oppressor.

I remember a friend I had many years ago, her name was Lettie. Her father had plenty of money and supplied her mother and herself with food and clothes, but no luxuries.

We went to Art School together, and all the students would buy reproductions of the "Winged Victory," "Whister's Mother" or something to bring art into their homes.

My friend's father called all these things "plunder." He would say, "Don't bring home any plunder."

So she lived a colorless life without a "Winged Victory" on her bureau or "Whistler's Mother on the wall.

He would say often to my friend and her mother, "When I die, you'll both be well off."

One day someone said to Lettie, "When are you going abroad?" (all art students went abroad.)

She replied, cheerfully, "Not 'till Papa dies."

So people always look forward to being free from lack and oppression.

Let us now free ourselves from the *tyrants of negative thinking.* We have been slaves to doubts, fears and apprehension and let us be delivered as Moses delivered the Children of Israel and come out of the Land of Egypt, out of the House of Bondage.

Find the thought which is your great oppressor; find the *King-Pin*.

In the logging camps in the Spring, the logs are sent down the rivers in great numbers.

Sometimes the logs become crossed and cause a jam. The men look for the log causing the jam (they call it the King-Pin), straighten it, and the logs rush down the river again.

Maybe your King-Pin is resentment. Resentment holds back your good.

The more you resent, the more you will have to resent; you grow a resentment track in your brain, and your expression will be one of habitual resentment.

You will be avoided and miss the golden opportunities which await you each day.

I remember a few years ago, the streets were filled with men selling apples.

They got up early to get the good corners.

I passed one several times on Park Avenue. He had the most disagreeable expression I have ever seen.

As people passed he said, "Apples! Apples!" but no one stopped to buy.

I invested in an apple and said, "You'll never sell apples unless you change your expression."

He replied, "Well that guy over there took my corner."

I said, "Never mind about the corner, you can sell apples right here if you'll look pleasant."

He said, "O.K. lady," and I went on. The next day I saw him, his whole expression had changed. He was doing a big business selling apples with a smile.

So find your king-pin (you may have more than one); and your logs of *success, happiness and abundance will go rushing down your river.*

"Go therefore now and work,
for there shall no straw be given you,
yet ye shall make bricks without straw."

NOTES

Manifesting Blueprint Form

To print duplicate Manifesting Blueprint Forms, go to the web: ww.SoulKisses.com/success

Part 1 - Choose to be Happy

After processing through the insight and energetic support of these three lectures review your biggest, happiest, most magnificent life energy again. When you open your heart to the limitless possibility that you are and DREAM Big - Outrageously BIG - is the energy the same as it was the first time you experienced this exercise?

Write in the section below what your ***biggest, happiest, most magnificent life*** feels like and looks like now (if you know what it looks like, but be open to something bigger and better ;)). Again, if you cannot "see" it, do not worry - you can definitely "FEEL" what you want your life to BE - and it may be more or even something different than what you experienced in Section I - especially if you are taking a week between lectures to process through the energetic expansion. Explore what makes your heart sing with joy and write about it here. You'll discover insights, clarity and a deeper knowing energy that you did not experience before.

My Biggest, Happiest, Most Magnificent Life:

_____

_____

_____

_____

_____

_____

_____

_____

_____

_____

_____

_____

_____

_____

_____

_____

_____

Part 2 - Fearlessly decide what you want and Celebrate experiencing it

Decide on one thing you want to manifest. It can be a new experience, something material or a relationship. It can be the same thing you wrote about in SECTION I or something different - you may have received what you set your intention to manifest in SECTION I. If you have not yet manifested your desire from SECTION I continue your focused attention to experiencing it. You'll feel the energy of the experience getting deeper and more stable within you - plus any energy that is between you and creating what you want will be revealed.

However, you may set an intention through the Manifesting Blueprint form to manifest something else. (You may print more copies of the form from the website: www.SoulKisses.com/success)

Remember, you do NOT need to know what you want will "look" like, but you MUST know what it will feel like to be, do or have it. If you know what you want looks like, be sure to include "this or better."

Declare what you want as an affirmation. An affirmation is an energy container of words that is supported by the energy of your beliefs. It is a declaration of what you wish to experience written with positive verbiage as if it has already happened.

Also include the Safety Clause: *"for the highest good of all - thank you, thank you, thank you."*

While writing, shift into the energy of what it will feel like to BE, DO or HAVE what you want - joyfully celebrate the experience. Shift till you feel a FULL - Body - YES energy within you!

Set your intention to manifest what you want and focus your attention to the excited energy experiencing what you want will give you:

_____

_____

_____

_____

_____

_____

_____

_____

_____

_____

_____

_____

_____

_____

Affirmation: _____

_____

Part 3 - Transform resistant fear energy to Love or Above

Address - immediately - any resistance energy that is revealed to you.

Be sure to update your Transformation Tool list so they will be at your fingertips when you need them.

When you identify the resistance energy in your body, ask your angels to "show you" where the uncomfortable energy stems from. Be aware that sometimes simply facing this energy is enough to dissipate it. If you need further assistance to transform this energy, Kate has a surplus of tools on the Soul Kisses Spiritual Whispers website to assist you (www.SoulKisses.com) and some of those tools are free, like the Essential Mastery Tools.

Write about this experience here:

Angels, show me where this resistance energy stems from: _____

_____

_____

_____

_____

_____

_____

_____

_____

_____

_____

_____

_____

_____

_____

_____

_____

_____

_____

_____

_____

_____

_____

Transformation Tool(s) I used to dissolve the resistance energy and what I experienced: _____

_____

_____

_____

_____

_____

_____

_____

_____

_____

_____

_____

_____

_____

_____

My most powerful Transformation Tools are: _____

_____

_____

_____

_____

_____

_____

_____

_____

_____

_____

_____

_____

_____

_____

_____

_____

_____

Part 4 - Demand and execute Action Steps

Demand Action Steps (if there are any) to bring to fruition what you wish to experience and be open to the guidance from within and from without as a hunch or intuition.

Action Steps I executed to manifest what I want:

Action Step 1: Maintain the excited energy of receipt - celebrate!

Part 5 - Prepare to receive.

Prepare to receive what you wish to be, do or have *when there is no sign of it in sight* and experience the CELEBRATION energy of receiving it as much as humanly possible.

Write down what you are doing to prepare and celebrate.

Remember, prepare for what you want to experience even when there is no sign of it in sight!

Preparation actions:

_____

_____

_____

_____

_____

_____

_____

_____

_____

_____

_____

_____

_____

_____

_____

_____

_____

_____

_____

_____

_____

_____

_____

SECTION III - Powerfully Manifest Through Your Energy

It is through your energy that you create your life experiences. YOU create your life experiences - life does NOT just happen to you! The following lectures, *Catch Up to Your Good, The Watchman at the Gate,* and *I Shall Never Want* support you to powerfully shift your energy from deep within to create a higher outcome.

You will take Albert Einstein's quote: *"We can't solve problems by using the same kind of thinking we used when we created them."* to a new level of experience as you shift your thinking from the subconscious beliefs within you to a higher vibration of knowing.

When you shift your energy - AND Maintain It as-much-as-humanly-possible - you transform your reality from the inside --- out!

The next three lectures will powerfully open the way for you to firmly anchor your new energetic state of BE-ing.

Action Step 1 - Florence's Teachings Speak to Me Powerfully

Read through the chapters of Florence's lectures in this section and highlight what speaks to you. After the chapter, use the NOTES page to write about why the highlighted sections resonated with you. Explore through writing what was revealed to you about your thought patterns and beliefs. Make note of the energy of hope and possibility you feel in your body and embrace that energy.

Important Action Step: Write about what spoke to you the most and how it is relevant to your life today.

Note: When you read Florence's teachings, your internal vibration of energy will ascend. With this ascension, resistance energy (your subconscious not being in agreement with your now conscious, aware state) will be revealed. Be sure to address any resistance energy that is revealed to you by using your tools. (If you are a student of the GAME of LIFE Mastery Program, be sure to access the Dynamic Mastery Tool Library.)

Action Step 2 - Manifesting Affirmation Container

Humans understand the structure of containers - containers hold things.

Affirmations are powerful, miraculous, magical energy containers. However, ---make note of this, it is very important!!! -- affirmations are ONLY powerful when they are in alignment with the energy of your innermost (subconscious) beliefs.

If an affirmation is out of alignment with your subconscious beliefs, you will feel it in your body - you'll feel resistance. If this is the case, look within and follow those uncomfortable breadcrumbs to the source and dissipate its power by facing it, disconnecting from it and healing it. And again, sometimes facing it is all you need to do. If there is a stronger pull there, use your Transformation Tools to shift into the Love or Above energy.

Read through this section, then return here to write powerful affirmations that embody the receipt of what you wish to manifest. You may write several or stick to one. But be SURE you feel a Full-Body-YES! when you say the affirmation. Then use sticky notes or other reminders to prompt you throughout your day to BE the energy of what you wish to manifest.

Ask your angels to help you form the words that fully convey your powerful manifesting energy. *ABOVE -- ALL -- ELSE -- the energy is what is MOST Important!*

My Powerful Affirmations

_____

_____

_____

_____

_____

_____

_____

_____

_____

_____

_____

_____

_____

_____

_____

_____

_____

_____

_____

_____

_____

RECAP

Consciously monitoring your energy to maintain Love or Above energy as much as humanly possible transforms your life. Through this conscious experience you will develop the "eyes to see" miracles spontaneously occurring for you.

What miracles have occurred for you thus far?

And... how are you progressing with your Daily Success Ritual to consciously set your intention each day? Are you finding it easier?

Write about your discoveries here:

_____

_____

_____

_____

_____

_____

_____

_____

_____

_____

_____

_____

_____

_____

_____

_____

_____

_____

_____

_____

_____

_____

_____

_____

_____

_____

_____

_____

_____

_____

Catch Up with Your Good

"And it shall come to pass,
that before they call, I will answer;
and while they are yet speaking, I will hear." - Isaiah 65:24

Catch up with your good! This is a new way of saying, "Before they call, I will answer."

Your good *precedes* you; it gets there before you do. But how to catch up with your good? For you must have ears that hear, and eyes that see, or it will escape you.

Some people never catch up with their good in life; they will say, "My life has always been one of hardship, no good luck ever comes to me." They are the people who have been asleep to their opportunities; or through laziness, haven't caught up with their good.

A woman told a group of friends that she had not eaten for three days. They dashed about asking people to give her work; but she refused it. She explained that she never got up until twelve o'clock, she liked to lie in bed and read magazines.

She just wanted people to support her while she read "Vogue" and "Harper's Bazaar." We must be careful not to slip into lazy states of mind.

Take the affirmation, "*I am wide awake to my good, I never miss a trick.*" Most people are only half awake to their good.

A student said to me, "If I don't follow my hunches, I always get into a jam."

I will tell the story of a woman, one of my students, who followed her intuitive leads which brought amazing results.

She had been asked to visit friends in a nearby town. She had very little money. When she arrived at her destination, she found the house locked up. They had gone away. She was filled with despair, then commenced to pray. She said, "Infinite Intelligence, give me a definite lead, let me know just what to do!"

The name of a certain hotel flashed into her consciousness, it persisted, the name seemed to stand out in big letters.

She had just enough money to get back to New York and the hotel. As she was about to enter, an old friend suddenly appeared, who greeted her warmly and whom she hadn't seen in years.

She explained that she was living at the hotel but was going away for several months, and added, "Why don't you live in my suite while I am away, it won't cost your a cent."

My friend accepted gratefully, and looked with amazement on the working of Spiritual Law.

She had caught up with her good by following intuition.

All going forward comes from desire. Science today, is going back to Lamarck and his "wishing theory." He claims that birds do not fly because they have wings, but they have wings because they wanted to fly; the result of the "push of the emotional wish."

Think of the irresistible power of thought with clear vision. Many people are in a fog most of the time, making wrong decisions and going the wrong way.

During the Christmas rush, my maid said to a saleswoman at one of the big shops, "I suppose this is your busiest day." She replied, "Oh no! The day *after* Christmas is our busiest day, when people bring most of the things back."

Hundreds of people choosing the wrong gifts because they were not listening to their intuitive leads.

No matter what you are doing, ask for guidance. It saves time and energy and often a lifetime of misery.

All suffering comes from the violation of intuition. Unless intuition builds the house, they labor in vain who build it.

Get the *habit of hunching*, then you will always be on the magic path.

"And it shall come to pass, that before they call, I will answer, and while they are yet speaking, I will hear."

Working with spiritual law, we are bringing to pass that which already is. In the Universal Mind it is there as an idea, but is crystallized on the external, by a sincere desire.

The idea of a bird was a perfect picture in divine mind, the fish caught the idea, and wished themselves into birds.

Are your desires bringing you wings? *We should all be bringing some seemingly impossible thing to pass.*

One of my affirmations is, *"The unexpected happens, my seemingly impossible good now comes to pass."*

Do not magnify obstacles, magnify the Lord - that means, magnify God's power.

The average person will dwell on all the obstacles and hindrances which are there to prevent his good coming to pass.

You "combine with what you notice," so if you give obstacles and hindrances your undivided attention, they grow worse and worse.

Give God your undivided attention. Keep saying silently (in the face of obstacles), *"God's ways are ingenious, His methods are sure."*

God's power is invincible, (though invisible). "Call unto me and I will answer thee, and show thee great and mighty things which thou knowest not."

In demonstrating our good, we must look away from adverse appearances, "Judge not by appearances."

Get some statement which will give you a feeling of assurance, *"The long arm of God reaches out over people and conditions, controlling the situation and protecting my interests!"*

I was asked to speak the word for a man who was to have a business interview with a seemingly unscrupulous person. I used the statement, and rightness and justice came out of the situation, at just the exact time I was speaking.

We have all heard the quotation from Proverbs, "Hope deferred maketh the heart grow sick, but when the desire cometh, it is a tree of life."

In desiring sincerely (without anxiety), we are catching up with the thing desired and the desire becomes crystallized on the external. "I will give to you the righteous desire of your heart.

Selfish desires, desires which harm others, always return to harm the sender.

The righteous desire might be called, an echo from the Infinite. It is already a perfect idea in divine mind.

All inventors catch up with the ideas of the articles they invent. I say in my book, "The Game of Life and How to Play It," the telephone was seeking Bell.

Often two people discover the same inventions at the same time. They have tuned in with the same idea.

The most important thing in life, is to bring the divine plan to pass.

Just as the picture of the oak is in the acorn, the divine design of your life is in your superconscious mind, and you must work out the perfect pattern in your affairs. You will then lead a magic life, for in the divine design, all conditions are permanently perfect.

People defy the divine design when they are asleep to their good.

Perhaps the woman who liked to lie in bed most of the day and read magazines should be writing for magazines but her habits of laziness dulled all desire to go forward.

The fishes who desired wings, were alert and alive, they did not spend their days on the bed of the ocean, reading "Vogue" and "Harper's Bazaar."

Awake thou that sleepeth and catch up with your good!

"Call on me and I will answer thee, and show thee great and mighty things, which thou knowest not."

"I now catch up with my good, for before I called I was answered."

NOTES

The Watchman at the Gate

"Also I set watchmen over you, saying, Hearken to the sound of the trumpet." - Jeremiah 6:17

We must all have a watchman at the gate of our thoughts. The Watchman at the Gate is the superconscious mind.

We have the power to choose our thoughts.

Since we have lived in the race thought for thousands of years, it seems almost impossible to control them. They rush through our minds like stampeding cattle or sheep.

But a single sheep-dog can control the frightened sheep and guide them into the sheep pen.

I saw a picture in the news-reels of a shepherd dog controlling the sheep. He had rounded up all but three. These three resisted and resented. They baahed and lifted their front feet in protest, but the dog simply sat down in front and never took his eyes off them. He did not bark or threaten. He just sat and looked his determination. In a little while the sheep tossed their heads and went in the pen.

We can learn to control our thoughts in the same way, by gentle determination, not force.

We take an affirmation and repeat it continually, while our thoughts are on the rampage.

We cannot always control our thoughts, but we *can control our words,* and repetition impresses the subconscious, and we are then master of the situation.

In the sixth chapter of Jeremiah we read: "I set a watchman over you, saying, Hearken to the sound of the trumpet."

Your success and happiness in life depend upon the watchman at the gate of your thoughts, sooner or later, crystallize on the external.

People think by running away from a negative situation, they will be rid of it, but the same situation confronts them wherever they go.

They will meet the same experiences until they have learned their lessons. This idea is brought out in the moving picture, "The Wizard of Oz."

The little girl, Dorothy, is very unhappy because the mean woman in the village wants to take away her dog, Toto.

She goes, in despair, to confide in her Aunt Em and Uncle Henry, but they are too busy to listen, and tell her to "run along."

She says to Toto, "There is somewhere, a wonderful place high above the skies where everybody is happy and no one is mean." How she would love to be there!

A Kansas cyclone suddenly comes along, and she and Toto are lifted up, high in the sky, and land in the country of Oz.

Everything seems very delightful at first, but soon she has the same old experiences. The mean old woman of the village has turned into a terrible witch, and is still trying to get Toto from her.

How she wishes she could be back in Kansas.

She is told to find the Wizard of Oz. He is all powerful and will grant her request.

She starts off to find his palace in the Emerald City.

On the way she meets a scarecrow. He is so unhappy because he hasn't a brain.

She meets a man made of tin, who is so unhappy because he hasn't a heart.

Then she meets a lion who is so unhappy because he has no courage.

She cheers them up by saying, "We'll all go to the Wizard of Oz and he'll give what we want" - the scarecrow a brain, the tin man a heart, and the lion courage.

They encounter terrible experiences, for the bad witch is determined to capture Dorothy and take away Toto and the ruby slippers which protect her.

At last they reach the Emerald Palace of the Wizard of Oz.

They ask for an audience, but are told no one has ever seen the Wizard of Oz, who lives mysteriously in the palace.

But through the influence of the good witch of the North, they enter the palace. There they discover the Wizard is just a fake magician from Dorothy's home town in Kansas.

They are all in despair because their wishes cannot be granted!

But then the good witch shows them that their wishes are *already* granted. The scarecrow has developed a brain by having to decide what to do in the experiences he has encountered, the tin man finds he has a heart because he loves Dorothy, and the lion has become courageous because he *had* to show courage in his many adventures.

The good witch from the North says to Dorothy, "What have you learned from your experiences?" and Dorothy replies, "I have learned that my heart's desire is in my own home and in my own front yard." so the good witch waves her wand, and Dorothy is at home again.

She wakes up and finds that the scarecrow, the tin man, and the lion are the men who work on her uncle's farm. They are so glad to have her back. This story teaches *that if you run away your problems will run after you.*

Be *undisturbed* by a situation, and it will fall away of its own weight.

There is an occult law of indifference. "None of these things move me." "None of these things disturb me" we might say in modern language.

When you can no longer be disturbed, all disturbance will disappear from the external.

"When your eyes have seen your teachers, your teachers disappear."

"I set watchmen over you, saying, Hearken to the sound of the trumpet."

A trumpet is a musical instrument, used in olden times, to draw people's attention to something - to victory, to order.

You will form the habit of giving attention to every thought and word, when you realize their importance.

The imagination, the scissors of the mind, is constantly cutting out the events to come into your life.

Many people are cutting out fear-pictures. Seeing things which are not divinely planned.

With the "single eye," man sees only the Truth. He sees through evil, knowing that out of it comes good. He transmutes injustice into justice, and disarms his seeming enemy by sending *goodwill*.

We read in mythology of the Cyclops, a race of giants, said to have inhabited Sicily. These giants had only one eye in the middle of the forehead.

The seat of the imaging faculty is situated in the forehead (between the eyes). So these fabled giants came from this idea.

You are indeed a giant when you have a single eye. Then every thought will be a constructive thought, and every word, a word of Power.

Let the third eye be the watchman at the gate.

"If therefore thine eye be single, thy whole body is full of light."

With the single eye your body will be transformed into your spiritual body, the "body electric" made in God's likeness and image (imagination).

By seeing clearly the perfect plan, we could redeem the world, with our *inner eye* seeing a world of peace and plenty and goodwill.

"Judge not by appearances, judge righteous judgment."

"Nation shall not lift up sword against nation, neither shall they learn war anymore."

The occult law of indifference means that you are undisturbed by adverse appearances. You hold steadily to the *constructive thought, which wins out.*

Spiritual law transcends the law of Karma.

This is the attitude of mind which must be held by the healer or practitioner towards his patient.

Indifferent to appearances of lack, loss or sickness, he brings about the change in mind, body and affairs.

Let me quote from the thirty-first chapter of Jeremiah. The keynote is one of rejoicing. It gives a picture of the individual freed from negative thinking.

"For there shall be a day that the watchmen upon the mount Ephraim shall cry, Arise ye, and let us go up to Zion unto the Lord our God."

The Watchman at the Gate neither slumbers nor sleeps. It is the "Eye which watches over Israel."

But the individual, living in a world of negative thought, is not conscious of this inner eye.

He may occasionally have flashes of intuition or illumination, then falls back into a world of chaos.

It takes determination and eternal vigilance to check up on words and thoughts. Thoughts of fear, failure, resentment and ill-will must be dissolved and dissipated.

Take the statement: "Every plant my father in heaven has not planted shall be rooted up."

This gives you a vivid picture of rooting up weeds in a garden. They are thrown aside, and dry up because they are without soil to nourish them.

You nourish negative thoughts by giving them your attention. Use the occult law of indifference and refuse to be interested.

Soon you will starve out the "army of all aliens." Divine ideas will crowd your consciousness, false ideas fade away, and you will desire only that which God desires through you.

The Chinese have a proverb, "The philosopher leaves the cut of his coat to the tailor."

So leave the plan of your life to the Divine Designer, and you will find all conditions permanently perfect.

The ground I am on is holy ground.
I now expand rapidly into the divine plan of my life,
where all conditions are permanently perfect.

NOTES

I Shall Never Want

"The Lord is my Shepherd; I shall not want." --Psalms 23:1

The 23rd Psalm is the best known of all the Psalms -- we might say that it is the keynote to the message of the bible.

It tells man he shall never want, when he has the realization (or conviction) that the Lord is his Shepherd; the realization that Infinite Intelligence supplies every need.

If you get this conviction today, every need will be met now and forever-more. You will draw, instantly, from the abundance of the spheres, whatever you desire or require; for what you need is *already on your pathway*.

A woman suddenly had the realization: "The Lord is my Shepherd, I shall never want." She seemed to be touching her invisible supply, she felt outside of Time and Space, she no longer relied on the external.

Her first demonstration was a small, but necessary one. She needed at once, some large paperclips, but had no time to go to the stationers to buy them.

In looking for something else, she opened a little-used chest, and in it, she found about a dozen large paperclips. She felt that the law was working, and gave thanks; then some needed money appeared, things large and small came her way.

Since then she has relied upon the statement: "The Lord is my Shepherd, I shall never want."

We used to hear people say, "I do not think it is right to ask God for money or things."

They did not realize that this Creative Principle is within each man. True Spirituality is proving God as your supply, daily, not just once in awhile.

Jesus Christ knew this law, for whatever he desired or required, appeared immediately on his pathway, the loaves and fishes and money from the fish's mouth.

With this realization, all hoarding and saving would disappear.

This does not mean that you should not have a bank account, and investments, but it does mean that you should not depend upon them, for if you had a loss in one direction, you would have a gain in another.

Always "your barns would be full and your cup flow over."

Now, how does one make this contact with his invisible supply? By taking a statement of Truth which clicks and gives him realization.

This is not open to a chosen few, "Whosoever calleth on the name of the Lord shall be delivered." The Lord is *your* shepherd and *my* shepherd and *everybody's* shepherd.

God is the Supreme Intelligence devoted to supplying man's need; the explanation is, that man is God in action. Jesus Christ said, "I and the Father are one."

We might paraphrase the statement and say, I and the great Creative Principle of the Universe, are one and the same.

Man only lacks when he loses his contact with this Creative Principle, which must be fully trusted, for it is Pure Intelligence and knows the way of Fulfillment.

The reasoning mind and personal will, cause a short circuit.

"Trust in me and I will bring it to pass."

Most people are filled with apprehension and dread, when there is nothing to cling to on the external.

A woman came to a practitioner and said, "I'm only a poor little woman with no one but God back of me." The practitioner said, "You need not worry if you have God back of you," for "all that the Kingdom affords is yours."

A woman called me on the phone and said, almost in tears, "I'm so worried about the business situation." I replied, "The situation with God remains the same: The Lord is your Shepherd, you shall not want." "If one door shuts, another door opens."

A very successful businessman who conducts all affairs on Truth methods said, "The trouble with most people is, that they get to relying on certain conditions. They haven't enough imagination to go forward - to open new channels."

Nearly every big success is built upon a failure.

I was told that Edgar Bergen lost his part in a Broadway production because they did not want any more dummies. Noel Coward got him on the Rudy Vallee radio hour, and he and Charlie McCarthy became famous over night.

I told the story, at one of my meetings of a man who was so poor and discouraged that he ended it all. A few days later came a letter notifying him that he had inherited a large fortune.

A man in the meeting said, "That means, when you want to be dead, your demonstration is three days off." Yes, *do not be fooled by the darkness before the dawn.*

It is a good thing to see the dawn once in a while, to convince you how unfailing it is. It reminds me of an experience of several years ago.

I had a friend who lived in Brooklyn near Prospect Park. She liked to do unusual things and said to me, "Come to visit me and we'll get up early and see the sunrise in Prospect Park."

At first I refused, and then came the hunch that it would be an interesting experience.

It was in the summer. We got up about four o'clock, my friend, her little daughter and myself. It was pitch dark, but we sallied forth down the street, to the entrance of the Park.

Some policemen eyed us curiously, but my friend said to them with dignity, "We are going to see the sunrise" and it seemed to satisfy them. We walked through the park to the beautiful rose garden.

A faint pink streak appeared in the East, then suddenly we heard a most tremendous uproar. We were near the Zoo and all the animals were greeting the dawn.

The lions and tigers roared, the hyenas laughed, there were shrieks and howls, every animal had something to say for a new day was at hand.

It was indeed most inspiring. The light slanted through the trees; everything had an unearthly aspect.

Then, as it grew lighter, our shadows were in front instead of behind us. The dawn of a new day!

This is the wonderful dawn which comes to each one of us, after some darkness.

Your dawn of Success, Happiness and Abundance is sure to come.

Every day is important, for we read in the wonderful Sanskrit poem, "Look well, therefore, to this day, such is the salutation of the dawn."

This day the Lord is your Shepherd! *This day,* you shall not want, as you and this great Creative Principle are one and the same.

The 34th Psalm is also a Psalm of security. It starts with a blessing for the Lord, "I will bless the Lord at all times, His praise shall continually be in my mouth."

"They that seek the Lord shall not want any good thing." Seeking the Lord means that man must make the first move. "Draw near to me and I will draw near to thee, saith the Lord."

You seek the Lord by making your affirmations, expecting and preparing for your good.

If you ask for success and prepare for failure, you will receive the thing you have prepared for.

I tell in my book, "The Game of Life and How to Play It," of a man who asked me to speak the word that all his debts be wiped out.

After the treatment, he said, "Now I'm thinking what I'll say to the people when I haven't the money to pay them." A treatment won't help you if you haven't faith in it, for faith and expectancy impresses the subconscious mind with the picture of fulfillment.

In the 23rd Psalm we read, "He restoreth my soul." Your soul is your subconscious mind and must be re-stored with the right ideas.

Whatever you feel deeply is impressed upon the subconscious, and manifests in your affairs.

If you are convinced that you are a failure, you will be a failure, until you impress the subconscious with the conviction you are a success.

This is done by making an affirmation which "clicks."

A friend in a meeting said that I had given her the statement as she was leaving the room, *"The ground you are on is harvest ground."* Things with her had been very dull, but this statement clicked.

"Harvest Ground, Harvest Ground," rang in her ears. Good things immediately commenced to come to her, and happy surprises.

The reason it is necessary to make an affirmation is because repetition impresses the subconscious. You cannot control your thoughts at first, but you can control your words, and Jesus Christ said, "By your *words* you are justified and by your *words* you are condemned."

Every day choose the right words, the right thoughts!

The Imaging faculty is the creative faculty, "Out of the imaginations of the heart come the issues of life."

We have all a bank we can draw upon, the Bank of the Imagination.

Let us imagine ourselves rich, well and happy. Imagine all our affairs are in divine order, but leave the way of fulfillment to Infinite Intelligence.

"He has weapons ye know not of." He has channels which will surprise you.

One of the most important passages in the 23rd Psalm is, "Thou preparest a table before me in the presence of mine enemies."

This means that even in the presence of the enemy situation, brought on by your doubts, fears or resentments, a way out is prepared for you.

The Lord is my Shepherd, I shall never want.

NOTES

Manifesting Blueprint Form

To print duplicate Manifesting Blueprint Forms, go to the web: ww.SoulKisses.com/success

Part 1 - Choose to be Happy

After processing through the insight and energetic support of the lectures in this section, review your biggest, happiest, most magnificent life energy again. As you process through the ascension energy you've been experiencing, both physically and spiritually, your perception of life events also shifts and ascends. You will find yourself to be calmer, more stable in your emotions. This doesn't mean you don't care. It means.... you're maintaining your power.

Write in the section below what your ***biggest, happiest, most magnificent life*** feels like and looks like today. Be aware of any resistance that is revealed and address it right away in the next sections.

My Biggest, Happiest, Most Magnificent Life:

_____

_____

_____

_____

_____

_____

_____

_____

_____

_____

_____

_____

_____

_____

_____

_____

_____

_____

_____

_____

Part 2 - Fearlessly decide what you want and Celebrate experiencing it

Look at what you've been working at manifesting in your previous Manifesting Blueprint Forms.

Use this form to expand that energy or set and anchor the intention with clarity and focus to manifest what you want and perhaps to manifest something new.

Remember, you do NOT need to know what it will "look" like, but you MUST know what it will feel like. If you know what you want looks like, be sure to include "this or better."

Create your affirmation energy container to help you anchor the energy of what you wish to experience and maintain that energy every time you use the affirmation.

Affirm "aright" as Florence says: *This or something better, by divine right, under grace in a miraculous way.*

Be sure to use the safety clause: *for the highest good of all!*

And include the love or above energy of gratitude: *thank you, thank you, thank you!*

While writing, shift into the energy of what it will feel like to be, do or have what you want - joyfully celebrate the experience. Shift till you feel a FULL - Body - YES energy within you!

Set your intention to manifest what you want and focus your attention to the excited energy experiencing what you want will give you:

_____

_____

_____

_____

_____

_____

_____

_____

_____

_____

_____

_____

_____

_____

_____

_____

Affirmation:_____

_____

_____

Part 3 - Transform resistant fear energy to Love or Above

When you shift from deep within, any energy that is not in alignment with what you want to experience will be revealed to you in the form of resistant energy in your body.

When you feel that resistance energy, ask your angels to "show you" where it stems from and follow through the process of facing it, disconnecting from it and healing it. If you need further assistance to transform this energy, Kate has a surplus of tools on the Soul Kisses Spiritual Whispers website to assist you.

Write about this experience here:

Angels, show me where this resistance energy stems from: _____

_____

_____

_____

_____

_____

_____

_____

_____

_____

_____

_____

_____

_____

_____

_____

_____

_____

_____

_____

_____

Transformation Tool(s) I used to dissolve the resistance energy and what I experienced: _____

_____

_____

_____

_____

_____

_____

_____

_____

_____

_____

_____

_____

_____

_____

_____

_____

_____

My most powerful Transformation Tools are: _____

_____

_____

_____

_____

_____

_____

_____

_____

_____

_____

_____

_____

_____

_____

_____

_____

_____

_____

Part 4 - Demand and execute Action Steps

Demand Action Steps (if there are any) to bring to fruition what you wish to experience and be open to the guidance from within and from without as a hunch or intuition.

Action Steps I executed to manifest what I want:

Action Step 1: Maintain the excited energy of receipt - celebrate!

Part 5 - Prepare to receive.

Prepare to receive what you wish to be, do or have *when there is no sign of it in sight* and experience the CELEBRATION energy of receiving it as much as humanly possible.

Have FUN preparing!

Remember, you're not faking it till you make it - you're setting the wheels in motion and anchoring their momentum to manifest what you want.

Preparation actions:

_____

_____

_____

_____

_____

_____

_____

_____

_____

_____

_____

_____

_____

_____

_____

_____

_____

_____

_____

_____

_____

_____

_____

_____

_____

_____

_____

_____

_____

SECTION IV - The Shift from Trust to Knowing

The next two lectures, *The Fork in the Road* and *Look with Wonder,* hold the energy of shifting from deep within from Trust to Knowing.

The shift from "Trust" to "Knowing" is a magical experience - an experience you won't forget. However, you may not recognize the moment it happens, but you will be astounded when you realize the shift has happened for you.

We read and are taught about having "faith and trusting," but little time is focused on teaching us how to understand "Knowing."

When you shift from faith and trust to "Knowing" all doubt is erased. You will feel stability from deep within you - a stability and decisiveness - ***Knowing*** - with every cell of your BE-ing that what you wish to experience "IS" happening even when there is no sign of it in site in your physical world!

You will KNOW from deep within that you are worthy, deserving and good enough to BE, DO and HAVE anything you want.

No more questioning, no more doubt - just ***matter of fact Knowing!***

You will have shifted to a new way of BE-ing - make it your new NORMAL way of BE-ing by staying there - in the knowing as much as humanly possible.

Action Step 1 - Florence's Teachings Speak to Me Powerfully

Read through the chapters of Florence's lectures in this section and highlight what speaks to you. After the chapter, use the NOTES page to write about why the highlighted sections resonated with you. Explore through writing what was revealed to you about your thought patterns and beliefs. Make note of the energy of hope and possibility you feel in your body and embrace that energy.

Important Action Step: Write about what spoke to you the most and how it is relevant to your life today.

Note: When you read Florence's teachings, your internal vibration of energy will ascend. With this ascension, resistance energy (your subconscious not being in agreement with your now conscious, aware state) will be revealed. Be sure to address any resistance energy that is revealed to you by using your tools. (If you are a student of the GAME of LIFE Mastery Program, be sure to access the Dynamic Mastery Tool Library.)

Action Step 2 - What do you believe about yourself?

What do you believe about yourself? Do you believe you're worthy? Deserving? Good enough? Lovable? Let me tell you - you ARE worthy, deserving, good enough and lovable. I, Kate Large, know this with every cell of my BE-ing - no matter what you have or have not done, you ARE worthy, deserving, good enough and lovable. I believe this unconditionally.

What do you believe?

We've discussed the "ins" and "outs" of resistance - what it is, what it means, how important it is to moving forward in our lives and what we need to do with it.

Ask yourself the following questions and write your belief about yourself. Discern if you feel any resistance in your body when you answer "yes" to the questions. If you experience any resistance, please, take the time to ask your angels to show you the core energy of the resistance and face it, disconnect from it and heal it. If you need a human hand of support, reach out to a trusted loving source. (If you do not have one, Kate offers private session on the www.SoulKisses.com website that may be perfect for you.)

Remember... humans are as an onion and there are many layers and levels of our understanding. These layers are an energetic vibration. The closer to love and above energy you are, the more clearly any negative belief about yourself will be revealed. Know this energy is not being revealed to punish you. It's begging to be healed.

If something is revealed that you thought you already processed through, know that you did process through it to the level of your vibration at the time. Now you are at a higher vibration and more of the core energy is being revealed - AND now, you know what to do with it!

Do I believe I'm worthy? _____

_____

_____

_____

_____

_____

_____

_____

_____

_____

_____

_____

_____

_____

_____

_____

_____

_____

Do I believe I'm deserving? _____

_____

_____

_____

_____

_____

_____

_____

_____

_____

_____

_____

_____

_____

_____

_____

_____

_____

_____

_____

_____

_____

_____

_____

_____

_____

_____

_____

_____

_____

_____

_____

_____

_____

Do I believe I'm good enough? _____

_____

_____

_____

_____

_____

_____

_____

_____

_____

_____

_____

_____

_____

_____

_____

_____

_____

_____

_____

_____

_____

_____

_____

_____

_____

_____

_____

_____

_____

_____

_____

Do I believe I'm lovable? _____

_____

_____

_____

_____

_____

_____

_____

_____

_____

_____

_____

_____

_____

_____

_____

_____

_____

_____

_____

_____

_____

_____

_____

_____

_____

_____

_____

_____

_____

_____

_____

_____

RECAP

Are you practicing your Daily Success Ritual every day?

Setting your intention and focusing your attention on that intention every day leads to not only a more successful day, but perfects your energetic foundation for success at anything you wish to experience.

You only have to experience this once to never want to go back to outside energies of people, places and situations ruling the experiences of your life.

What about resistance energy? Now you know what it is and what it feels like, are you facing it when it reveals itself to you?

When you read something and are really wowed by it - resonating with the energy of it, but then don't implement it into your daily activity, nothing changes - life stays the same. It is of vital importance that you *IMPLEMENT* what you are taking in.

YOU are a powerful, limitless spiritual BE-ing!

Embrace your power and transform your life by shifting your energy to the love or above vibration of joy that experiencing what you want will give you. Reading this, then laying it down won't change your life, but shifting your energy to a higher vibration and maintaining your energy WILL.

Create and use magical Affirmation Containers! When you instill a Full - Body - YES! energy into your affirmations and use them consistently, you set the wheels in motion to manifest what you want.

And what you want.... becomes inevitable!

_____
_____
_____
_____
_____
_____
_____
_____
_____
_____
_____
_____
_____
_____
_____

The Fork in the Road

"Choose you this day whom ye will serve." - Joshua 24:15

Every day there is a necessity of choice (a fork in the road).

"Shall I do this, or shall I do that? Shall I go, or shall I stay?" Many people do not know what to do. They rush about letting other people make decisions for them, then regret having taken their advice.

There are others who carefully reason things out. They weigh and measure the situation like dealing in groceries, and are surprised when they fail to obtain their goal.

There are still other people who follow the magic path of intuition and find themselves in their Promised Land in the twinkling of an eye.

Intuition is a spiritual faculty high above the reasoning mind, but on the path is all that you desire or require.

In my book "The Game of Life and How to Play It," I give many examples of success attained through using this marvelous faculty. I say also that prayer is telephoning to God and intuition is God telephoning to you. (Correspondence Course.)

So choose ye this day to follow the magic path of intuition.

In my question and answer classes I tell you how to cultivate intuition.

In most people it is a faculty which has remained dormant. So we say, "Awake thou that sleepeth. Wake up to your leads and hunches. Wake up to the divinity within!"

Claude Bragdon said, "To live intuitively is to live fourth dimensionally."

Now it is necessary for your to make a decision, you face a fork in the road. *Ask for a definite unmistakable lead,* and you will receive it.

We find many events to interpret metaphysically in the Book of Joshua. "After the death of Moses, the divine command came to Joshua, 'Now therefore, arise, go over the Jordan, thou and all thy people, unto the land which I do give to them. Every place the sole of your feet shall tread upon; to you have I given it'."

The feet are the symbol of understanding, so it means metaphysically all that we understand stands under us in consciousness, and what is rooted there can never be taken from us.

For, the bible goes on to say: "There shall not any man be able to stand before thee all the days of thy life... I will not fail thee, nor forsake thee. Only be thou strong and very courageous, that thou mayest observe to do according to all the law, which Moses my servant commanded thee: turn not from it to the right hand or to the left, that thou mayest prosper whithersoever thou goest."

So we find we have success through being strong and very courageous in following spiritual law. We are back again to the "fork in the road" - the necessity of choice.

"Choose you this day whom ye shall serve," the intellect or divine guidance.

A well-known man, who has become a great power in the financial world, said to a friend, "I always follow intuition and I am luck incarnate."

Inspiration (which is divine guidance) is the most important thing in life. People come to Truth meetings for inspiration. I find the right word will start divine activity operating in their affairs.

A woman came to me with a complication of affairs. I said to her, "Let God juggle the situation." It clicked. She took the affirmation, "I now let God juggle this situation." Almost immediately she rented a house, which had been vacant for a long time.

Let God juggle every situation, for when you try to juggle the situation, you drop all the balls.

In my question and answer classes, I would be asked, "how do you let God juggle a situation, and what do you mean when you say I should not juggle it?"

You juggle with the intellect. The intellect would say, "Times are hard, no activity in real estate. Don't expect anything until the Fall of 1958."

With spiritual law there is only the *now*. Before you call you are answered, for "time and space are but a dream," and *your blessing is there waiting for you to release it by faith and the word.*

"Choose you this day whom ye will serve," fear or faith.

In every act prompted by fear lies the germ of its own defeat.

It takes much strength and courage to trust God. We often trust him in little things, but when it comes to a big situation we feel we had better attend to it ourselves; then comes defeat and failure.

The following extract from a letter which I received from a woman in the West shows how conditions can change in the twinkling of an eye.

"I've had the pleasure of reading your wonderful book, 'The Game of Life and How to Play It.' I have four boys, ten, thirteen, fifteen and seventeen, and thought how wonderful for them to grasp it, in their early life, and be able to get things which are theirs by Divine Right.

"The lady who let me read her copy gave me other things to read, but it seemed when I picked this book up it was magnetic and I could not let go of it. After reading it I realized, I was trying to live Divinely but did not understand the law, or I would have been much further advanced.

"At first I thought it quite hard to find a place in the business world, after so many years of being a mother. But I got this statement, *'God makes a way where there is no way.'* And He did that very thing for me.

"I am grateful for my position, and smile when people say, 'How do you do it, manage four growing boys, a home, after all the times you have been hospitalized with such major operations and none of your relatives near you?'"

I have that statement in my book, *"God makes a way where there is no way."*

God made a way for her in business when all her friends said it couldn't be done.

The average person will tell you almost anything can't be done.

I had an example of this the other day. In a shop I found a delightful little silver dripolator which would make just one cup of anything. I showed it to some friends with enthusiasm, thinking it so very cute, and one said, "It will never work." The other said, "If it belonged to me, I'd throw it away." I stood up for the little dripolator and said I knew it would work, which it did.

My friends were simply typical of the average person who says, "It can't be done."

All big ideas meet with opposition.

Do not let other people rock your boat.

Follow the path of wisdom and understanding, "and turn not from it to the right hand or to the left, that thou mayest prosper whithersoever thou goest."

In the thirteenth verse of the twenty-fourth chapter of Joshua, we read a remarkable statement: "And I have given you a land for which ye did not labour, and cities which ye built not, and ye dwell in them; of the vineyards and olive yards which ye planted not, do ye eat."

This shows that man cannot *earn* anything, his blessings come as gifts. (Gifts lest any man shall boast.)

With the *realization of wealth,* we receive the gift of wealth.

With the *realization of success,* we receive the gift of success, for success and abundance are states of mind.

"For it is the Lord our God, he it is, that brought us up, and our fathers out of the land of Egypt, out of the house of bondage."

The land of Egypt stands for darkness - the house of bondage, where man is a slave to his doubts and fears, and beliefs in lack and limitation, the result of having followed the wrong fork in the road.

Misfortune is due to failure to stick to the things which spirit has revealed through intuition.

All big things have been accomplished by men who stuck to their big ideas.

Henry Ford was past middle age when the idea of the Ford car came to him. He had great difficulty in raising the money. His friends thought it was a crazy idea. His father said to him, tearfully, "Henry, why do you give up a good twenty-five dollar a week job in order to chase a crazy idea?" But no one could rock Henry Ford's boat.

So in order to come out of the land of Egypt, out of the land of bondage, we must make the right decisions.

Follow the right fork in the road. "Only be thou strong and very courageous, that thou mayest observe to do according to the law, which Moses my servant commanded thee: turn not from it to the right hand nor to the left, that thou mayest prosper whithersoever thou goest."

So, as we reach the fork in the road today, let us fearlessly follow the voice of intuition.

The bible calls it "the still small voice."

"There came a voice behind me, saying, 'This is the way, walk ye in it'."

On this path is the good, already prepared for you.

You will find the "land for which ye did not labour, and cities which ye built not, and ye dwell in them; of the vineyards and oliveyards which ye planted not, do ye eat."

I am divinely led,
I follow the right fork in the road.
God makes a way where there is no way.

NOTES

Look with Wonder

"I will remember the works of the Lord; surely I will remember thy wonders of old." - Psalms 77:11

The words wonder and wonderful are used many times in the Bible. In the dictionary the word wonder is defined as, "a cause for surprise, astonishment, a miracle, a marvel."

Ouspensky, in his book, "Tertium Organum," calls the 4th dimensional world, the "World of the Wondrous." He has figured out mathematically, that there is a realm where all conditions are perfect. Jesus Christ called it the Kingdom.

We might say, "Seek ye first the world of the wondrous, and all things shall be added unto you."

It can only be reached through a state of consciousness.

Jesus Christ said, to enter the Kingdom we must become "as a little child." Children are continually in a state of joy and wonder!

The future holds promises of mysterious good. Anything can happen overnight.

Robert Louis Stevenson, in "A Child's Garden of Verses" says: "The world is so full of a number of things. I'm sure we should all be as happy as kings."

So let us look with wonder at that which is before us; that statement was given me a number of years ago, I mention it in my book, "The Game of Life and How To Play It."

I had missed an opportunity and felt that I should have been more awake to my good. The next day, I took the statement early in the morning, *"I look with wonder at that which is before me."*

At noon the phone rang, and the proposition was put to me again. This time I grasped it. I did indeed, look with wonder for I never expected the opportunity to come to me again.

A friend in one of my meetings said the other day, that this statement had brought her wonderful results. It fills the consciousness with happy expectancy.

Children are filled with happy expectancy until grown-up people, and unhappy experiences bring them out of the world of the wondrous!

Let us look back and remember some of the gloomy ideas which were given us: "Eat the speckled apples first." "Don't expect too much, then you won't be disappointed." "You can't have everything in this life." "Childhood is your happiest time." "No one knows what the future will bring." What a start in life!

These are some of the impressions I picked up in early childhood.

At the age of six I had a great sense of responsibility. Instead of looking with wonder at that which was before me, I looked with fear and suspicion. I feel much younger now than I did when I was six.

I have an early photograph taken about that time, grasping a flower, but with a careworn and hopeless expression.

I had left the world of the wondrous behind me! I was now living in the world of realities, as my elders told me and it was far from wondrous.

It is a great privilege for children to live in this age, when they are taught Truth from their birth.

Even if they are not taught actual metaphysics, the ethers are filled with joyous expectancy.

You may become a Shirley Temple or a Freddy Bartholomew or a great pianist at the age of six and go on a concert tour.

We are all now back in the world of the wondrous, where anything can happen overnight, for when miracles do come, they come quickly!

So let us become *Miracle Conscious* and prepare for miracles, expect miracles, and we are then inviting them into our lives.

Maybe you need a financial miracle! There is a supply for every demand. Through active faith, the word and intuition, we release this invisible supply.

I will give an example: One of my students found herself almost without funds, she needed one thousand dollars, and she had had plenty of money at one time and beautiful possessions, but had nothing left but an ermine wrap. No fur dealer would give her much for it.

I spoke the word that it would be sold to the right person for the right price, or that the supply would come in some other way. It was necessary that the money manifest at once, it was no time to worry or reason.

She was on the street making her affirmations. It was a stormy day. She said to herself, "I'm going to show active faith in my invisible supply by taking a taxi cab." It was a very strong hunch. As she got out of the taxi, at her destination, a woman stood waiting to get in.

It was an old friend, a very, very kind friend. It was the first time in her life she had ever taken a taxi, but her Rolls Royce was out of commission that afternoon.

They talked and my friend told her about the ermine wrap. "Why," her friend said, "I will give you a thousand dollars for it." And that afternoon she had the cheque.

God's ways are ingenious, His methods are sure.

A student wrote me the other day, that she was using that statement - *God's ways are ingenious, His methods are sure.* A series of unexpected contacts brought about a situation she had been desiring. She looked with wonder at the working of the law.

Our demonstrations usually come within a "split second." All is timed with amazing accuracy in Divine Mind.

My student left the taxi, just as her friend stopped to enter; a second later, she would have hailed another taxi.

Man's part is to be wide awake to his leads and hunches; for on the magic path of Intuition is all that he desires or requires.

In Moulton's Modern Reader's Bible, the book of Psalms is recognized as the perfection of lyric poetry.

"The musical meditation which is the essence of lyrics can find no higher field than the devout spirit which at once raises itself to the service of God, and overflows on the various sides of active and contemplative life."

The Psalms are also human documents, and I have selected the 77th Psalm because it gives the picture of a man in despair, but as he contemplates the wonders of God, faith and assurance are restored to him.

"I cried unto God with my voice, even unto God with my voice; and He gave ear unto me. In the day of my trouble I sought the Lord: my soul refused to be comforted. Will the Lord cast off forever? And will he be favourable no more? Hath God forgotten to be gracious? Hath he in anger shut up his tender mercies? And I said, This is my infirmity, but I will remember the years of the right hand of the Most High. I will remember the works of the Lord; surely I will remember the wonders of old. I will meditate also of all thy work, and talk of thy doings. Thy way, O God, is in the sanctuary: who is so great a God as our God! Thou art the God that doest wonders. Thou hast with thine arm redeemed thy people."

This is a picture of what the average Truth student goes through when confronted with a problem. He is assailed by thoughts of doubt, fear and despair.

Then some statement of Truth will flash into his consciousness - "God's ways are ingenious, His methods are sure!" He remembers other difficulties which have been overcome, his confidence in God returns. He thinks, *"what God has done before, He will do for me and more!"*

I was talking to a friend not long ago who said, "I would be pretty dumb if I didn't believe God could solve my problem. So many times before, wonderful things have come to me, I know they will come again!"

So the summing up of the 77th Psalm is, "What God has done before, he now does for me and more!"

It is a good thing to say when you think of your past success, happiness or wealth. All loss comes from your own vain imaginings, fear of loss crept into your consciousness, you carried burdens and fought battles, you reasoned instead of sticking to the magic path of intuition.

But in the twinkling of an eye, all will be restored to you, for as they say in the East, "What Allah has given, cannot be diminished."

Now to go back to the child's state of consciousness, you should be filled with wonder, but be careful not to live in your past childhood.

I know people who can only think about their happy childhood days. They remember what they wore! No skies have since been so blue, or grass so green. They therefore miss the opportunities of the wonderful now.

I will tell an amusing story of a friend who lived in a town when she was very young, then moved away to another city. She always looked back to the house they first lived in, to her it was an enchanted palace, large, spacious and glamorous.

Many years after, when she had grown up, she had an opportunity of visiting this house. She was disillusioned, she found it small, stuffy and ugly. Her idea of beauty had entirely changed, for in the front yard was an iron dog.

If you went back to your past, it would not be the same. So in this friend's family, they called living in the past, "iron dogging."

Her sister told me a story of some "iron dogging" she had done. When she was about sixteen, she met abroad, a very dashing and romantic young man, an artist. This romance didn't last long, but she talked about it a lot to the man she afterwards married.

Years rolled by, the dashing and romantic young man, had become a well-known artist and came to this country to have an exhibition of his pictures. My friend was filled with excitement, and hunted him up to renew their friendship. She went to his exhibition, and in walked a portly business man, no trace was left of the dashing romantic youth! When she told her husband, all he said was, "iron dogging."

Remember, *now* is the appointed time! *Today* is the day! *And your good can happen over night.*

Look with wonder at that which is before you!

We are filled with divine expectancy, "I will restore to you the years which the locusts have eaten!"

Now let each one think of the good which seems so difficult to attain. It may be health, wealth, happiness or perfect self-expression.

Do not think *how* your good can be accomplished, just give thanks that you have already received on the invisible plane, "therefore the steps leading up to it are secured also."

Be wide awake to your intuitive leads, and suddenly, you find yourself in your Promised Land.

"I look with wonder at that which is before me."

NOTES

Manifesting Blueprint Form

To print duplicate Manifesting Blueprint Forms, go to the web: ww.SoulKisses.com/success

Part 1 - Choose to be Happy

It's time to review your biggest, happiest, most magnificent life energy again. If you've processed through the information and exercises thus far through your heart space and implemented Florence's teachings, you've made tremendous progress.

You've identified the tell tale signs of resistance energy and now fully understand how valuable it is. And most importantly, you know what to do to process through it to reclaim your love or above energy and maintain it - making what you want to experience *inevitable!*

When you revisit what you wish to manifest, allowing yourself to DREAM Big - Outrageously BIG - are you finding it easier to reach that incredible opulent feeling of joy?

Are you seeing the less than love worry, fear energy for what it is... an illusion?

Are you keeping your Worry Angel employed? (meet him with your Free Essential Mastery Tools at www.SoulKisses.com)

Write in the section below what your ***biggest, happiest, most magnificent life*** feels like and looks like now after processing through Florence's teaching lectures. Be aware of any resistance that is revealed and address it right away in the next sections.

My Biggest, Happiest, Most Magnificent Life:

_____

_____

_____

_____

_____

_____

_____

_____

_____

_____

_____

_____

_____

_____

_____

Part 2 - Fearlessly decide what you want and Celebrate experiencing it

Look at what you've been working at manifesting in your previous Manifesting Blueprint Forms.

Use this form to expand that energy or set and anchor the intention with clarity and focus to manifest something new that you want.

Create your affirmation energy container to help you anchor the energy of what you wish to experience and maintain that energy every time you use the affirmation.

Affirm "aright" as Florence says: *This or something better, by divine right, under grace in a miraculous way* and include Dr. Anne Marie Evers' safety clause: *for the highest good of all!* plus use the love or above energy of gratitude: *thank you, thank you, thank you!*

While writing, shift into the energy of what it will feel like to be, do or have what you want - joyfully celebrate the experience. Shift till you feel a FULL - Body - YES energy within you!

Set your intention to manifest what you want and focus your attention on the excited energy experiencing what you want will give you:

_____

_____

_____

_____

_____

_____

_____

_____

_____

_____

_____

_____

_____

_____

_____

_____

_____

_____

_____

_____

Affirmation: _____

_____

_____

_____

Part 3 - Transform resistant fear energy to Love or Above

Transforming resistant fear energy to Love or Above is a living breathing experience. You will discover that some tools are more powerful for you than others. And this will change as you grow and evolve. Be open to the guidance within you as to which method of transforming the energy will work best.

Be sure to update your Transformation Tool list so they will be at your fingertips when you need them.

When you identify the resistance energy in your body, ask your angels to "show you" where the uncomfortable energy stems from. If you need further assistance to transform this energy, Kate has a surplus of tools on the Soul Kisses Spiritual Whispers website as programs, services and products to assist you.

Write about this experience here:

Angels, show me where this resistance energy stems from: _____

_____

_____

_____

_____

_____

_____

_____

_____

_____

_____

_____

_____

_____

_____

_____

_____

_____

_____

_____

Transformation Tool(s) I used to dissolve the resistance energy and what I experienced: _____

_____

_____

_____

_____

_____

_____

_____

_____

_____

_____

_____

_____

_____

My most powerful Transformation Tools are: _____

_____

_____

_____

_____

_____

_____

_____

_____

_____

_____

_____

_____

_____

Part 4 - Demand and execute Action Steps

Demand Action Steps (if there are any) to bring to fruition what you wish to experience and be open to the guidance from within and from without as a hunch or intuition.

Action Steps I executed to manifest what I want:

Action Step 1: Maintain the excited energy of receipt - celebrate!

_____

_____

_____

_____

_____

_____

_____

_____

_____

_____

_____

_____

_____

_____

_____

_____

_____

_____

_____

_____

_____

_____

_____

_____

_____

_____

_____

_____

_____

Part 5 - **Prepare to receive.**

Prepare to receive what you wish to be, do or have *when there is no sign of it in sight* and experience the CELEBRATION energy of receiving it as much as humanly possible.

Preparation actions:

_____

_____

_____

_____

_____

_____

_____

_____

_____

_____

_____

_____

_____

_____

_____

_____

_____

_____

_____

_____

_____

_____

_____

_____

_____

_____

_____

_____

_____

_____

_____

_____

NOTES

SECTION V - Out-Picturing Beliefs as Prosperity

You create your reality through the energy within you - all that you judge as: the good, the bad, and the ugly. The next lectures, *The Long Arm of God* and *The Secret Door to Success* fully support you to burst through that glass ceiling of limitation to experience the joy, love and happiness that is your birthright.

So many times, we know we want something better than what we have, but we don't know what it is. By shifting your energy to the joy and elation of BE-ing Happy, you open the door for wonderful, exciting experiences of prosperity to manifest through you.

Florence's teachings hold the energy for you to embrace to Out-Picture, or manifest, your new beliefs, and those new beliefs are founded in the prosperity energy of the Love or Above vibration.

Action Step 1 - Florence's Teachings Speak to Me Powerfully

Read through the chapters of Florence's lectures in this section and highlight what speaks to you. After the chapter, use the NOTES page to write about why the highlighted sections resonated with you. Explore through writing what was revealed to you about your thought patterns and beliefs. Make note of the energy of hope and possibility you feel in your body and embrace that energy.

Important Action Step: Write about what spoke to you the most and how it is relevant to your life today.

Note: When you read Florence's teachings, your internal vibration of energy will ascend. With this ascension, resistance energy (your subconscious not being in agreement with your now conscious, aware state) will be revealed. Be sure to address any resistance energy that is revealed to you by using your tools. (If you are a student of the GAME of LIFE Mastery Program, be sure to access the Dynamic Mastery Tool Library.)

Action Step 2 - Accurate Guidance

Revisit your Manifestation Blueprint and discern if anything needs to be tweaked or updated. Are you maintaining your energy of receipt? Celebrating receipt?

Ignoring resistance energy? If you're ignoring resistance energy, don't beat yourself up, just face it, disconnect from it and heal it. Remember, sometimes simply facing it is enough to disconnect and heal it. If you're having trouble, you don't have to do this alone. Kate has many opportunities available for you to get additional support on the www.SoulKisses.com website if you do not currently know someone who will support you.

What action steps are your taking to prepare to receive?

DEMAND a lead to show you any action steps you are to take and don't let the universe off the hook! Allow yourself to have the eyes to see, the ears to hear and the ability to understand easily the knowing guidance of your heart.

Write here what you discover, the action steps you need to take, and the outcome:

_____

_____

_____

_____

_____

_____

_____

_____

_____

_____

_____

_____

_____

_____

_____

_____

_____

_____

_____

_____

_____

_____

_____

_____

_____

_____

_____

_____

_____

_____

_____

_____

RECAP

You are a limitless spiritual BE-ing! You deserve to be, do and have everything that makes your heart sing with joy! I know this - and now, you know from deep within your heart that this is true.

Continue to updated and perfect your Daily Success Ritual. As you grow and expand your awareness moving into the love or above energy of Christ Consciousness, you'll feel the need to update your daily ritual. Follow the guidance of your heart.

Continue to face resistance energy as quickly as you can when it is revealed to you. There will be a time that the deep, life changing resistance energy will be a thing of the past because you will have healed it.

Update your Affirmation Container mantras as your awareness expands to maintain the energy behind them as love or above.

Do not allow yourself to become distraught if you experience a contraction of your energy. This is normal and is a sign that you're expanding and stretching and moving into a new way of BE-ing - a new "Normal" way of experiencing your life - your magical life of love, joy and happiness in whatever form that takes for you.

Know that if you are fully supported by not only the Angelic realm, but the energies of Mother Earth as well. It is your mission, everyone's mission, to transcend the illusion of being limited and accept the truly limitless possibility that you are.

_____

_____

_____

_____

_____

_____

_____

_____

_____

_____

_____

_____

_____

_____

_____

_____

NOTES

_____

_____

_____

_____

_____

_____

_____

_____

_____

_____

_____

_____

_____

_____

_____

_____

_____

_____

_____

_____

_____

_____

_____

_____

_____

_____

_____

_____

_____

_____

_____

_____

_____

_____

_____

_____

The Long Arm of God

"The Eternal God is thy refuge, and underneath are the everlasting arms." - Deuteronomy 33:27

In the bible, the arm of God always symbolizes protection. The writers of the bible knew the power of a symbol. It brings a picture which impresses the subconscious mind. They used the symbols of the rock, sheep, shepherds, vineyard, lamp, and hundreds of others. It would be interesting to know how many symbols are used in the bible. The arm also symbolizes strength.

"The eternal God is thy refuge, and underneath are the everlasting arms, and he shall thrust out the enemy from before thee and shall say, Destroy them."

Who is the enemy "before thee"? The negative thought-forms which you have built up in your subconscious mind. A man's enemies are only those of his own household. The everlasting arms thrust out these enemy thoughts and destroy them.

Have you ever felt the relief of getting out some negative thought-form? Perhaps you have built up a thought-form of resentment, until you are always boiling with anger about something. You resent people you know, people you don't know, people in the past and people in the present, and you may be sure that the people in the future won't escape your wrath.

All the organs of the body are affected by resentment - for when you resent, you resent with every organ of the body. You pay the penalty with rheumatism, arthritis, neuritis, etc., for acid thoughts produce acid in the blood. All this trouble comes because you are fighting the battle, not leaving it to the long arm of God.

I have given the following statement to many of my students. *"The long arm of God reaches out over people and conditions, controlling this situation and protecting my interests.*

This brings a picture of a long arm symbolizing strength and protection. With the realization of the power of the long arm of God, you would no longer resist or resent. You would relax and let go. The enemy thoughts within you would be destroyed, therefore, *the adverse conditions would disappear.*

Spiritual development means the ability to stand still, or stand aside, and let Infinite Intelligence lift your burdens and fight your battles. When the burden of resentment is lifted, you experience a sense of relief! You have a kindly feeling for everyone, and all the organs of your body begin to function properly.

A clipping quoting Albert Edward Day, D.D. reads, "That loving our enemies is good for our spiritual health is widely known and accepted. But that negation and poisonous emotions destroy physical health, is a relatively new discovery. The problem of health is often an emotional one. Wrong emotions entertained and repeated are potent causes of illness. When the preacher talks about loving your enemies, the man on the street is apt to dismiss the idea as unendurable and pious. But the fact is, the preacher is telling you something which is one of the first laws of hygiene, as well as ethics. No man even for his body's sake can afford to indulge in hatred. It is like repeated doses of poison. When you are urged to get rid of fear, you are not listening to a moon-struck idealist; rather you are hearing counsel that is as significant for health as advice about diet."

We hear so much about a balanced diet, but without a balanced mind you can't digest what you eat, calories or no calories.

Non-resistance is an art. When acquired, The World is Yours! So many people are trying to force situations. Your lasting good will never comes through forcing personal will.

"Flee from the things which flee from thee,
Seek nothing, fortune seeketh thee.
Behold his shadow on the floor!
Behold him standing at the door!"

I do not know the author of these lines. Lovelock, the celebrated English athlete, was asked how to attain his speed and endurance in running. He replied, "Learn to relax." Let us attain this rest in action. He was most relaxed when running the fastest.

Your big opportunity and big success usually slide in, when you least expect it. You have to let go long enough for the *great law of attraction to operate. You never saw a worried and anxious magnet.* It stands up straight and hasn't a care in the world, because it knows needles can't help jumping to it. The things we rightly desire come to pass when we have taken the clutch off.

I say in my correspondence course, "*Do not let your heart's desire become your heart's disease." You are completely demagnetized when you desire something too intensely.* You worry, fear, and agonize. There is an occult law of indifference - "None of these things move me." *Your ships come in over a don't care sea.*

Many people in Truth antagonize friends, because they are too anxious for them to read the books and go to the lectures. They meet opposition.

A friend took my book, "The Game of Life and How to Play It" to her brother's house to read. The young men of the family refused to read it. No "nut stuff" for them. One of these young men drives a taxi cab. One night he drove a taxi which belonged to another man. In going over the car he found a book stuffed away somewhere. It was "The Game of Life and How to Play It." The next day he said to his aunt, "I found Mrs. Shinn's book in the taxi last night. I read it and it's great! There's a lot of good reading in it. Why doesn't she write another book?" God works in roundabout ways, his wonders to perform.

I meet unhappy people and a few grateful and contented people. A man said to me one day, "I have a great deal to be thankful for. I have good health, enough money and I'm still single!"

The eighty-ninth psalm is very interesting, for we find that two individuals take part, the man who sings the psalm (for all psalms are songs or poems), and Lord God of Hosts answers him. It is a song of praise and thanksgiving, extolling the strong arm of God.

"I will sing of the mercies of the Lord forever!"

"O Lord God of Hosts, who is a strong Lord like unto thee?"

"Thou hast a mighty arm, strong is thy hand, and high is thy right hand."

Then the Lord of Hosts replies:

"With whom my hand shall be established, mine arm also shall strengthen him."

"My mercy will I keep for him for evermore, and my covenant shall stand fast with him."

We only hear the words "for evermore" in the bible and in fairy-tales. In the absolute, man is outside of time and space. His good is "from everlasting to everlasting." The fairy-tales came down from the old Persian legends which were founded upon Truth.

Aladdin and His Wonderful Lamp is the out-picturing of the Word. Aladdin rubbed the lamp and all his desires came to pass. Your word is your lamp. Words and thoughts are a form of radio activity and do not return void. A scientist has said that words are clothed in light. *You are continually reaping the fruits of your words.*

A friend in one of my meeting said that she had brought a man to my class who had been out of work for a year or more. I gave the statement: *Now is the appointed time. Today is the day of my amazing good fortune.* It clicked in his consciousness. Soon after, he was given a position which paid him nine thousand dollars a year!

A woman told me that when I blessed the offering I said that each offering would return a thousand fold. She had put a dollar in the collection. She said with great realization, "That dollar is blessed and returns a thousand dollars." She received a thousand dollars a short time afterwards, in a most unexpected way.

Why do some people demonstrate this Truth so much more quickly than others? It is because they have the ears that hear. Jesus Christ tells the parable of the man who sowed the seed and it fell upon good ground. The seed is the word. I say, *"Listen for the statement that clicks; the statement that gives your realization. That statement will bear fruit."*

The other day I went into a shop where I know the employer quite well. I had given one of his employees an affirmation card. I said to him, jokingly, "I wouldn't waste an affirmation card on you. You wouldn't use it." He replied, "Oh sure, give me one. I'll use it." The following week I gave him a card. Before I left he rushed up to me excitedly and said, "I made the statement and two new customers walked in." It was: "Now is the appointed time; today is the day of my amazing good fortune." It had clicked.

So many people use their words in exaggerated and reckless statements. I find a great deal of material for my talks in the beauty parlor. A young girl wanted a magazine to read. She called to the operator, "Give me something terribly new and frightfully exciting." All she wanted was the latest moving picture magazine.

You hear people say, "I wish something terribly exciting would happen." They are inviting some unhappy, but exciting, experience into their lives. Then they wonder why it happened to them.

There should be a chair of metaphysics in all colleges. *Metaphysics is the wisdom of the ages.* It is the ancient wisdom taught all through the centuries in India and Egypt and Greece. Hermes Trismegistus was a great teacher of Egypt. His teachings were closely guarded and have come down to us over ten centuries. He lived in Egypt in the days when the present race of men was in its infancy. But if you read the "Kybalion" carefully, you find that he taught just what we are teaching today. He said that all mental states were accompanied by vibrations. You combine with what you vibrate to, so let us all now vibrate to success, happiness and abundance.

Now is the appointed time.
Today is the day of my amazing good fortune.

NOTES

The Secret Door to Success

"So the people shouted when the priests blew with the trumpets; and it came to pass,
when the people heard the sound of the trumpet,
and the people shouted with a great shout,
that the wall fell down flat, so that the people went up into the city,
every man straight before him, and they took the city."- Joshua 6:20

A successful man is always asked - "What is the secret of your success?"

People never ask a man who is a failure, "What is the secret of your failure?" It is quite easy to see and they are not interested.

People all want to know how to open the secret door to success.

For each man there is success, but it seems to be behind a door or wall. In the Bible reading, we have heard the wonderful story of the falling of the walls of Jericho.

Of course all biblical stories have a metaphysical interpretation.

We will talk now about your wall of Jericho: the wall separating you from success. Nearly everyone has built a wall around his own Jericho.

This city you are not able to enter, contains great treasures; your divinely designed success, your heart's desire!

What kind of wall have you built around your Jericho? Often, it is a wall of resentment - resenting someone, or resenting a situation, shuts off your good.

If you are a failure and resent the success of someone else, you are keeping away your own success.

I have given the following statement to neutralize envy and resentment.

What God has done for others, He now does for me and more.

A woman was filled with envy because a friend had received a gift, she made this statement, and an exact duplicate of the gift was given her - plus another present.

It was when the children of Israel shouted, that the walls of Jericho fell down. When you make an affirmation of Truth, your wall of Jericho totters.

I gave the following statement to a woman: *The walls of lack and delay now crumble away, and I enter my Promised Land, under grace.* She had a vivid picture of stepping over a fallen wall, and received the demonstration of her good, almost immediately.

It is the word of realization which brings about a change in your affairs; for words and thoughts are a form of radio-activity.

Taking an interest in your work, enjoying what you are doing opens the secret door of success.

A number of years ago I went to California to speak at the different centers, by way of the Panama Canal, and on the boat I met a man named Jim Tully.

For years he had been a tramp. He called himself The King of the Hoboes.

He was ambitious and picked up an education.

He had a vivid imagination and commenced writing stories about his experiences.

He dramatized tramp life, he enjoyed what he was doing, and became a very successful author. I remember one book called "Outside Looking In." It was made into a motion picture

He is now famous and prosperous and lives in Hollywood. What opened the secret door to success for Jim Tully?

Dramatizing his life - being interested in what he was doing, he made the most of being a tramp. On the boat, we all sat at the captain's table, which gave us a chance to talk.

Mrs. Grace Stone was also a passenger on the boat; she had written the "Bitter Tea of General Yen," and was going to Hollywood to have it made into a moving-picture; she had lived in China and was inspired to write the book.

That is the *Secret* of Success, to *make what you are doing interesting to other people*. Be interested yourself, and others will find you interesting.

A good disposition, a smile, often opens the secret door; the Chinese say, "A man without a smiling face, must not open a shop."

The success of a smile was brought out in a French moving-picture in which Chevalier took the lead, the picture was called, "With a Smile." One of the characters had become poor, dreary and almost a derelict; He said to Chevalier "What good has my honesty done me?" Chevalier replied, "Even honesty won't help you, without a smile." So the man changes on the spot, cheers up, and becomes very successful.

Living in the past, complaining of your misfortunes, builds a thick wall around your Jericho.

Talking too much about your affairs, scattering your forces, brings you up against a high wall. I knew a man of brains and ability, who was a complete failure.

He lived with his mother and aunt, and I found that every night when he went home to dinner, he told them all that had taken place during the day at the office; he discussed his hopes, his fears, and his failures.

I said to him, "You scatter your forces by talking about your affairs. Don't discuss your business with your family. Silence is golden!"

He took my lead. During dinner he refused to talk about business. His mother and aunt were in despair. They loved to hear all about everything, but his silence proved golden!

Not long after, he was given a position at one hundred dollars a week, and in a few years, he had a salary of three hundred dollars a week.

Success is not a secret, it is a System.

Many people are up against the wall of discouragement. Courage and endurance are part of the system. We read this in lives of all successful men and women.

I had an amusing experience which brought this to my notice. I went to a moving picture theatre to meet a friend.

While waiting, I stood near a young boy, selling programs.

He called to people passing, "Buy a complete program of the picture, containing photographs of the actors and a sketch of their lives."

Most people passed by without buying. To my great surprise, he suddenly turned to me, and said - "Say, this ain't no racket for a guy with ambition!"

Then he gave a discourse on success. He said, "Most people give up just before something big is coming to them. A successful man never gives up."

Of course I was interested and said, "I'll bring you a book the next time I come. It is called *The Game of Life and How to Play It*. You will agree with a lot of the ideas."

A week or two later I went back with the book.

The girl at the ticket office said to him - "Let me read it, Eddie, while you are selling programs." The man who took tickets leaned over to see what it was about.

"The Game of Life" always gets people's interests.

I returned to the theatre in about three weeks, Eddie had gone. He had expanded into a new job that he liked. His wall of Jericho had crumbled, he had refused to be discouraged.

Only twice, is the word success mentioned in the Bible -- both times in the Book of Joshua.

"Only be strong and very courageous to observe to do according to all the law which Moses, my servant, commanded thee: turn not from it to the right nor to the left, that thou mayest have good success whithersoever thou goest. This book of the law shall not depart from thy mouth, but thou shalt meditate therein day and night, that thou mayest observe to do all that is written therein, for then shalt thou make thy way prosperous and thou shalt have good success. Turn not to the right nor to the left."

The *road to success is a straight and narrow path; it is a road of loving absorption, of undivided attention.*

You attract the things you give a great deal of thought to.

So if you give a great deal of thought to lack, you attract lack, if you give a great deal of thought to injustice, you attract more injustice.

Joshua said, "And it shall come to pass, that when they make a long blast with the ram's horn, and when ye hear the sound of the trumpet, all the people shall shout with a great shout: and the wall of the city shall fall down flat, and the people shall ascend up, every man straight before him."

The inner meaning of this story, is the power of the word, your word which dissolves obstacles, and removes barriers.

When the people shouted the walls fell down.

We find in folk-lore and fairy stories, which come down from legends founded on Truth, the same idea - a word opens a door or cleaves a rock.

We have it again in the Arabian Night's Story, "Ali Baba and The Forty Thieves." I saw it made into a moving picture.

Ali Baba has a secret hiding place, hidden somewhere behind rocks and mountains, the entrance may only be gained by speaking a secret word. -- It is "Open Sesame!"

Ali Baba faces the mountain and cries - "Open Sesame!" and rocks slide apart.

It is very inspiring, for it gives you the realization of how YOUR own rocks and barriers, will part at the right word.

So let us take the statement --
The walls of lack and delay now crumble away,
and I enter my Promised Land, under grace.

NOTES

Manifesting Blueprint Form

To print duplicate Manifesting Blueprint Forms, go to the web: ww.SoulKisses.com/success

Part 1 - Choose to be Happy

It's time to review your biggest, happiest, most magnificent life energy again.

You've been shifting your energy to the highest state of love possible, identifying resistance, and disconnecting from it to take your power back.

The human "need" to control people and life situations is subsiding because now, you manage loving control, through the empowerment of love that is your essence. You're now able to accept your life as it is and if it isn't what you want, you know how to discern the energy of what you want, shift into it, use tools to anchor it and bring it to fruition ===> manifestation without anxiety - only love.

Are you keeping your Worry Angel employed? (meet him with your Free Essential Mastery Tools at www.SoulKisses.com)

Write in the section below what your *biggest, happiest, most magnificent life* feels like and looks like now after processing through Florence's teaching lectures. Be aware of any resistance that is revealed and address it immediately in the next sections.

My Biggest, Happiest, Most Magnificent Life:

_____

_____

_____

_____

_____

_____

_____

_____

_____

_____

_____

_____

_____

_____

_____

_____

Part 2 - Fearlessly decide what you want and Celebrate experiencing it

Look at what you've been working at manifesting in your previous Manifesting Blueprint Forms.

Use this form to expand that energy or set and anchor the intention with clarity and focus to manifest something new that you want.

Create your affirmation energy container to help you anchor the energy of what you wish to experience and maintain that energy every time you use the affirmation.

Affirm "aright" as Florence says: *This or something better, by divine right, under grace in a miraculous way* and include Dr. Anne Marie Evers' safety clause: *for the highest good of all!* plus use the love or above energy of gratitude: *thank you, thank you, thank you!*

While writing, shift into the energy of what it will feel like to be, do or have what you want - joyfully celebrate the experience. Shift till you feel a FULL - Body - YES energy within you!

Set your intention to manifest what you want and focus your attention on the excited energy experiencing what you want will give you:

_____

_____

_____

_____

_____

_____

_____

_____

_____

_____

_____

_____

_____

_____

_____

_____

_____

Affirmation:_____

_____

_____

_____

Part 3 - Transform resistant fear energy to Love or Above

Transforming resistant fear energy to Love or Above is a living breathing experience.

You've learned what manifesting tools work best for you. Be open to new ones coming your way.

Know that the tools you use to transform resistant energy are NOT "coping mechanisms." Your transformation tools do just that, transform energy from less than love to love or above and they are vitally important.

In the past, you used coping methods that only put a bandaid on your pain. Now you have the skills and tools to support you to truly heal from deep within so you can BE your authentic self: Love and Limitless Possibility - One with The Creator of All That Is.

Be sure to update your Transformation Tool list so they will be at your fingertips when you need them.

When you identify the resistance energy in your body, ask your angels to "show you" where the uncomfortable energy stems from. If you need further assistance to transform this energy, Kate has a surplus of tools on the Soul Kisses Spiritual Whispers website as programs, services and products to assist you.

Write about this experience here:

Angels, show me where this resistance energy stems from: _____

_____

_____

_____

_____

_____

_____

_____

_____

_____

_____

_____

_____

_____

_____

_____

_____

_____

Transformation Tool(s) I used to dissolve the resistance energy and what I experienced: _____

_____
_____
_____
_____
_____
_____
_____
_____
_____
_____
_____
_____
_____

My most powerful Transformation Tools are: _____

_____
_____
_____
_____
_____
_____
_____
_____
_____
_____
_____
_____
_____
_____
_____

Part 4 - Demand and execute Action Steps

Demand Action Steps (if there are any) to bring to fruition what you wish to experience and be open to the guidance from within and from without as a hunch or intuition.

Action Steps I executed to manifest what I want:

Action Step 1: Maintain the excited energy of receipt - celebrate!

Part 5 - Prepare to receive.

Prepare to receive what you wish to be, do or have *when there is no sign of it in sight* and experience the CELEBRATION energy of receiving it as much as humanly possible.

Preparation actions:

_____

_____

_____

_____

_____

_____

_____

_____

_____

_____

_____

_____

_____

_____

_____

_____

_____

_____

_____

_____

_____

_____

_____

_____

_____

_____

_____

_____

_____

_____

NOTES

SECTION VI - Positioned for Success - Your New Life

Through the past few weeks, if you've completed the exercises in this book, you've achieved energetic clarity of what you wish to experience as the reality of your life. You've shifted your vibration to the love or above energy and worked with your Angelic A-Team to face, disconnect from and heal the resistance energy that was revealed.

As you've processed through this book, you've learned that your Manifesting Blueprint is a living breathing plan to make manifesting the life your heart desires effortless.

As a living breathing plan, it is necessary to keep it updated as you learn new techniques and methods to process through resistance energy.

You've been rewriting neural pathways of belief and setting wheels into motion to live your biggest, most magnificent life - no matter what is going on around you.

You are positioning yourself for the ultimate success story:

Living Your Version of Heaven on Earth!

Action Step 1 - Florence's Teachings Speak to Me Powerfully

Read through the chapters of Florence's lectures in this section and highlight what speaks to you. After the chapter, use the NOTES page to write about why the highlighted sections resonated with you. Explore through writing what was revealed to you about your thought patterns and beliefs. Make note of the energy of hope and possibility you feel in your body and embrace that energy.

Important Action Step: Write about what spoke to you the most and how it is relevant to your life today.

Note: When you read Florence's teachings, your internal vibration of energy will ascend. With this ascension, resistance energy (your subconscious not being in agreement with your now conscious, aware state) will be revealed. Be sure to address any resistance energy that is revealed to you by using your tools. (If you are a student of the GAME of LIFE Mastery Program, be sure to access the Dynamic Mastery Tool Library.)

Action Step 2 - Maintaining Your Power

Read the two lectures in this section, *Crossing Your Red Sea* and *The Inner Meaning of Snow White and the Seven Dwarfs,* and complete Action Step 1.

Then revisit each of your Manifesting Blueprints and review the expansion of your core energy.

Have you determined and listed the Transformation Tools that work the best for you?

What do you wish to manifest next? You may print additional copies of the Manifesting Blueprint here: www.SoulKisses.com/success

Fine tune your Daily Success Ritual to support what you wish to manifest.

Be open to new tools that come your way to make maintaining the expectant energy of receipt effortless! Be sure to add them to your Transformation Tool list.

Write about important action steps you've discovered that hold the most power for you here:

_____

_____

_____

_____

_____

_____

_____

_____

_____

_____

_____

_____

_____

_____

_____

_____

_____

_____

_____

_____

_____

_____

_____

_____

_____

_____

_____

_____

RECAP

Reading Florence's teachings empower you and support you to create miraculous experiences as you daily life.

You will discover that every time you pick up this book, you will discover something you did not see before. And the reason this happens is because you've ascended your energy and the energy of the words speak to you in a different way - a higher way than they did before.

Through your shift to the higher vibration of Love or Above energy you will be attracting to you new people and experiences that will bring you great prosperity, joy and happiness.

Be OPEN to the experience. Allow yourself to have the "eyes to see," the "ears to hear," and the "wisdom to accept the knowing in your heart."

Continue to implement, expand and improve your Daily Success Ritual to support you to maintain your Love or Above energetic vibration.

Crossing Your Red Sea

"Speak unto the children of Israel that they go forward." - Exodus 14:15

One of the most dramatic stories in the bible is the episode of the children of Israel crossing the Red Sea.

Moses was leading them out of the land of Egypt where they were kept in bondage and slavery. They were being pursued by the Egyptians.

The children of Israel, like most people, did not enjoy trusting God; they did a lot of murmuring. They said to Moses: "Is not this the word that we did tell thee in Egypt, saying, Let us alone, that we may serve the Egyptians? For it had been better for us to serve the Egyptians, than that we should die in the wilderness."

"And Moses said unto the people, Fear ye not, stand still, and see the salvation of the lord, which he will show to you today, for the Egyptians whom ye have seen today, ye shall see them again no more forever."

"The Lord shall fight for you, and ye shall hold your peace."

We might say that Moses pounded faith into the children of Israel.

They preferred being slaves to their old doubts and fears (for Egypt stands for darkness), than to take the giant swing into faith, and pass through the wilderness to their Promised Land.

There is, indeed, a wilderness to pass through before your Promised Land is reached.

The old doubts and fears encamp round about you, but, there is always someone to tell you to go forward! There is always a Moses on your pathway. Sometimes it is a friend, sometimes intuition!

"And the Lord said to Moses, Wherefore cryest though unto me? Speak unto the children of Israel, that *they go forward!*"

"But lift thou up thy rod, and stretch out thine hand over the sea, and divide it; and the children of Israel shall go on dry ground through the midst of the sea."

"And Moses stretched out his hand over the sea; and the Lord caused the sea to go back by a strong east wind all that night, and made the sea dry land, and the waters were divided."

"And the children of Israel went into the midst of the sea upon the dry ground, and the waters were a wall unto them on their right hand, and on their left."

"And the Egyptians pursued, and went in after them to the midst of the sea, even all Pharaoh's horses, his chariots, and his horsemen."

"And the Lord said unto Moses, Stretch out thine hand over the sea, that the waters may come again upon the Egyptians, upon their chariots, and upon their horsemen."

"And Moses stretched forth his hand over the sea, and the sea returned; and the Egyptians fled against it, and the Lord overthrew the Egyptians in the midst of the sea."

"And the waters returned, and covered the chariots, and the horsemen, and all the hosts of Pharaoh that came into the sea after them; there remained not so much as one of them."

Now remember, the bible is talking about the individual. It is talking about *your* wilderness, *your* Red Sea, and *your* Promised Land.

Each one of you has a Promised Land, a heart's desire, but you have been so enslaved by the Egyptians (your negative thoughts), it seems very far away, and too good to be true. You consider trusting God a very risky proposition. The wilderness might prove worse than the Egyptians.

And how do you know your Promised Land really exists?

The reasoning mind will always back up the Egyptians.

But sooner or later, something says, *"Go forward!"* It is usually circumstances -- you are driven to it.

I give the example of a student.

She is a very marvelous pianist and had great success abroad. She came back with a book full of press clippings, and a happy heart.

A relative took an interest in her and said she would back her financially for a concert tour. They chose a manager who took charge of the expenses, and attended to her bookings.

After a concert or two, there were no more funds. The manager had taken them. My friend was left stranded, desolate and disappointed. This was about the time that she came to me.

She hated the man, and it was making her ill. She had very little money and could afford only a cheerless room where her hands were often too cold to practice.

She was indeed, in bondage to the Egyptians -- hate, resentment, lack and limitation.

Someone brought her to one of my meetings, and she spoke to me and told her story.

I said, "In the first place you must stop hating that man. When you are able to forgive him, your success will come back to you. You are taking your initiation in forgiveness."

It seemed a pretty big order, but she tried and came regularly to all my meetings.

In the meantime, the relative had started a suit to recover the money. Time went on and it never came to court.

My friend had a call to go to California. She was no longer disturbed by the situation, and had forgiven the man.

Suddenly, after about four years, she was notified that the case had come to court. She called me upon her arrival in New York, and asked me to speak the word for rightness and justice.

They went at the time appointed, and it was all settled out of court, the man restoring the money by monthly payments.

She came to me overflowing with joy, for she said, "I hadn't the least resentment toward the man. He was amazed when I greeted him cordially." Her relative said that all the money was to go to her, so she found herself with a big bank account.

Now she will soon reach her Promised Land. She came out of the house of bondage (of hate and resentment) and crossed her Red Sea. Her goodwill toward the man caused the waters to part, and she crossed over on dry land.

Dry land symbolizes something substantial under your feet, the feet symbolizing understanding.

Moses stands out as one of the greatest figures in biblical history.

"It came to Moses to move from Egypt with his nation. The task before him was not only the unwillingness of Pharaoh to let go of those whom he had made into profitable slaves, but also to stimulate to open rebellion this nation which had lost its initiative under the hardships of its taskmasters."

"It required extraordinary genius to meet this condition, which Moses possessed with self abnegation and the courage of his own convictions. Self abnegation! He was called the meekest of men. We have often heard the expression, 'As meek as Moses.' He was so meek towards the commands of the Lord, that he became one of the strongest of men."

The Lord said to Moses, "lift thou up thy rod, and stretch out thine hand over the sea, and divide it: and the children of Israel shall go on dry ground through the midst of the sea."

So, never doubting, he said to the children of Israel, "Go forward." This was a daring thing to do, to lead a multitude of people into the sea, having perfect faith they would not drown.

Behold the miracle!

"... the Lord caused the sea to go back by a strong east wind all that night, and made the sea dry land, and the waters were divided."

Now remember, this could happen *for you* this very day. Think of your problem.

Maybe you have lost your initiative from living so long a slave to Pharaoh (your doubts, fears and discouragements).

Say to yourself, *"Go forward."*

" ... the Lord caused the sea to go back by a strong east wind."

We will think of this strong east wind as a strong affirmation.

Take a vital statement of Truth. For example if your problem is a financial one, say *"My supply comes from God, and big happy financial surprises now come to me, under grace, in perfect ways."* The statement is a good one, for it contains the element of mystery.

We are told that God works in mysterious ways His wonders to perform. We might say in surprising ways. Now that you have made your statement for supply, you have caused the east wind to blow.

So walk up to your Red Sea of lack or limitation. The way to walk up to your Red Sea is to do something to *show* your fearlessness.

I will tell the story of a student who had an invitation to visit friends at a very fashionable summer resort.

She had been living in the country for a long time, grown heavier, and nothing fitted her but her girl scout suit. Suddenly, she received the invitation. It meant evening clothes, slippers and accessories, none of which she had, and no money to buy them. She came to me. I said, "What is your hunch?"

She replied, "I feel very fearless. I have the hunch to go anyway."

So she squeezed herself into something to travel in and went.

When she arrived at her friend's house she was greeted warmly, but her hostess said, with some embarrassment, "Maybe what I've done will hurt you, but there are some evening clothes and slippers I never wear which I have put in your room. Won't you make use of them?"

My friend assured her she would be delighted -- and everything fitted perfectly.

She had, indeed, walked up to her Red Sea and passed over on dry land.

The waters of my Red Sea part,
and I pass over on dry land,
I now go forward into my Promised Land.

NOTES

The Inner Meaning of Snow White and the Seven Dwarfs

I have been asked to give a Metaphysical interpretation of Snow White and the Seven Dwarfs, one of Grimm's Fairy Tales.

It is amazing how this picture, a fairy story, swept sophisticated New York, and the whole country, due to Walt Disney's genius.

This fairy tale was supposed to be for children, but men and women have packed the theatre. It is because fairy tales come down from old legends of Persia, India and Egypt, which are founded on Truth.

Snow White, the little Princess, has a cruel stepmother, who is jealous of her. This cruel stepmother idea appears also in "Cinderella."

Nearly everyone has a cruel step-mother. THE CRUEL STEP-MOTHER IS A NEGATIVE THOUGHT-FORM YOU HAVE BUILT UP IN THE SUBCONSCIOUS.

Snow White's cruel step-mother is jealous of her and always keeps her in rags and in the background. ALL CRUEL THOUGHT FORMS DO THIS.

The cruel step-mother consults her magic mirror every day, saying: "Magic mirror on the wall, who is the fairest of them all?" One day the mirror replies: "Thou Queen, mayst fair and beauteous be, but Snow White is lovelier far than thee." This enrages the Queen, so she decides to send Snow White to the forest to be killed by one of her servants. However, the servant's heart melts when Snow White begs for her life, so he leaves her in the woods. The woods are filled with terrifying animals and many pitfalls and dangers. She falls in terror to the ground, and while there, a most unusual spectacle presents itself. Scores of the most delightful little animals and birds creep up and surround her. Rabbits, squirrels, deer, beavers, raccoons, etc. She opens her eyes and greets them with pleasure; they are so friendly and attractive. She tells her story and they lead her to a little house which she makes her home. NOW THESE FRIENDLY BIRDS AND ANIMALS SYMBOLIZE OUR INTUITIVE LEADS OR HUNCHES, WHICH ARE ALWAYS READY TO "GET YOU OUT OF THE WOODS."

The little house proves to be the home of the Seven Dwarfs. Everything is in disorder, so Snow White and her animal friends begin to clean the house. The squirrels dust with their tails, the birds hang things up, using the little deer's horns for a hat-rack. When the seven dwarfs come home from their work of digging gold, they discover the change and at last find Snow White asleep on one of the beds. In the morning she tells her story, remains with them to keep house and cook their meals, and is very happy. THE SEVEN DWARFS SYMBOLIZE THE PROTECTIVE FORCES ALL ABOUT US.

In the meantime, the cruel step-mother consults her mirror and it says to her: "Over the hills in the green wood shade, where the Seven Dwarfs their dwelling have made, there Snow White is hiding her head, and she, is lovelier far, Oh, Queen than thee." This infuriates the Queen; so she starts off disguised as an old hag, with a poisoned apple for Snow White. She finds her in the house of the Seven Dwarfs and tempts her with the big, red luscious apple. The birds and animals endeavor to tell her not to touch it. THEY TRY TO GIVE HER THE HUNCH NOT TO EAT IT. They rush around in dismay, but Snow White can't resist the apple, she takes one bite and falls, apparently dead. Now all the little birds and animals rush off to bring the Seven Dwarfs to the rescue; but too late, Snow White lies lifeless. They all bow their little heads in grief. Then suddenly the Prince appears, kisses Snow White, and she comes to life. They are married and live happily ever after. The Queen, the cruel step-mother, is swept away by a terrific storm, THE OLD THOUGHT-FORM IS DISSOLVED AND DISSIPATED FOREVER. THE PRINCE SYMBOLIZES THE DIVINE PLAN OF YOUR LIFE. WHEN IT WAKES YOU UP YOU LIVE HAPPILY EVER AFTER.

This is the fairy story which has enthralled New York and the whole country.

Find out what form of tyranny your cruel stepmother is taking in your subconscious. It is some negative conviction which works out in all your affairs.

We hear people saying: "My good always comes to me too late." "I've lost so many opportunities!" We must reverse the thought and say repeatedly: *"I am wide awake to my good, I never miss a trick."*

WE MUST DROWN OUT THE DREARY SUGGESTIONS OF THE CRUEL STEPMOTHER. *ETERNAL VIGILANCE IS THE PRICE OF FREEDOM FROM THESE NEGATIVE THOUGHT-FORMS.*

NOTES

Transformation Tools

Suggested tools to transform the fear energy of "resistance" to love or above energy:

Release the need to be a victim
Release unforgiveness
Release the need to feel unworthy
Release the need to feel undeserving
Release the need to believe you're unlovable
Open your heart to loving you
Look within and work with your angels
Shift your energy to love
Disconnect the cords energetically
EFT
Sedona Method of Release
Attitude of Gratitude
Discern where your energy leaks
Re-write your Subconscious Records (Neural Pathways of belief)
Ground into love energy
Tap into the energy of your Higher Self
Access your Field of Potentiality
Work with a trusted accountability partner
Read positive, self help books that resonate
Meditate
Journal
Work with your angels
Reclaim your power
Reiki
Theta Healing
Healing Touch

Tools Kate uses Soul Kisses Website:
These transformation tools and many more may be found on the Soul Kisses website: www.SoulKisses.com

Recorded Programs and Webinars
**Communicating with the Angels
**Create more Love in Your Life
**Disconnect the Cords to Heal the Wounds of Your Heart
**Give Yourself the Gift of Forgiveness
**How to Create Your Heaven on Earth
**Meet Your Money Angel
**Meet Your Worry Angel
**Prosperity Tool Kit
**How to Peek into Your Future During Mercury Retrograde
**Moon Cycle Blueprint for Prosperity
**Angels & New Moon Energy Reveal: Your Access to Prosperity Portal
**Angels & Full Moon Energy Reveal: Your Pathway to Miracles
**Affirmations: Your Passport to Happiness with Dr. Anne Marie Evers

Guided Journey Meditations
Healing Trilogy: Love, Worthiness, Forgiveness
Claim Your Power
Clear Your Chakras with the Healers of the Light

Tap into Your Higher Self
The Power of Gratitude
Shift Your Energy to Love
Healing Circle of Love

Recommended books of support:

** The Game of Life and How to Play It, by Florence Scovel Shinn

** The Game of Life Workbook, by Florence Scovel Shinn and Kate Large

** 10 Be's of Positivity, by Lynette Turner

** Affirmations, Your Passport to Happiness, by Dr. Anne Marie Evers

** The Seven Spiritual Laws of Success, by Deepak Chopra

** You Can Heal Your Life, by Louise Hay

** Conversations with God, by Neale Donald Walsch

** Angelspeake, How to Talk with Your Angels, by Trudy Griswold

** A Still, Small Voice, by Echo Bodine

** The Four Spiritual Laws of Prosperity, by Edwene Gaines

** E-Squared, by Pam Grout

    ** E-Cubed, by Pam Grout

More About Kate & Florence's Life Mastery Programs

Florence was born in 1871 and was a female forerunner of spiritual teachings. She lived in the male dominated world of the early 20th century - a time when new age metaphysical teachings were not mainstream.

Florence taught that the square of life is: health, wealth, love and perfect self-expression. She taught that perfecting the ability to consciously create within you and BE the energy of the end result you wish to achieve, were key to powerfully creating a new external experience - a new reality.

People listened, shifted their energy and proved her teachings to be spot on!

Norman Vincent Peale, author of *The Power of Positive Thinking*, said this about Florence's work: *"THE GAME OF LIFE is filled with wisdom and creative insights. That its teachings will work I know to be fact, for I've long used them myself. By studying and practicing the principles laid down in this book (The Game of Life and How to Play It) one may find prosperity, solve problems, have better health, achieve good personal relations—in a word, win the game of life!"*

Florence was a forerunner of teaching the power of the human energetic vibration through simplicity. She used case studies of her students to convey wisdom through practical examples, but the core magnificence of her teachings is the "energetic container" established for the learner! She taught that the energy of your words, the energy of your beliefs, and the energy of your BE-ing *is what creates your daily experience of life!*

Florence made The Law of Attraction (all the Universal Laws, really) easy to understand and master! She taught that the universe responds to you - *based on the vibration of your internal creation energy*. She explained with simplicity how to shift your internal energy through the vibratory container of your thoughts, words and beliefs.

These were radical teachings for a woman divorced in 1912. Florence's divorce accelerated her understanding of metaphysical principles and universal laws as she learned to create her own happiness from within - no matter what her circumstances looked like. As a result, she began to share her experiences with others and to teach. The energy of her students shifted within and their reality expanded into limitless possibility --- creating miraculous experiences!

Florence taught people how to shift their energy from within to expand their consciousness and transform the reality of their lives to something happier. Her students implemented her simple teachings and fulfilled their dreams and desires, not to mention their needs - no matter what was going on around them. ....And there was a LOT going on! Florence was headquartered in New York City where the US experienced the Great Depression and a recession, while the world was at war with World War I and II.

Florence was guided to write *The Game of Life and How to Play It*, but no publisher of the time would touch it - so in 1925 she self-published. The copyright has since expired.

Many publishers sell the book on Amazon today - in both paperback and kindle format. Even with digital downloads available, hundreds of thousands of hold-in-your-hand books are still sold every year.

The simple, timeless teachings of this short, easy to read book has supported millions of people in the past 100 years to ease their suffering and pain from the inside out to create higher outcomes as their reality.

In my opinion, the teachings of Florence Scovel Shinn are the *best kept secret of the 20th century!* A secret that's been kept from mainstream society for almost a 100 years. But for those who've discovered it, and consistently implemented it, they've created miraculous lives that they love!

Florence's books and teachings were on the new thought scene way before *The Secret*, Louise Hay, Wayne Dyer and Norman Vincent Peale - even before Napolean Hill's first book, *The Law of Success* that was published in 1928.

The Game of Life and How to Play It **has stood the test of time.**

How I met Florence

I was introduced to Florence in the early 90's. My rollercoaster life had been on a downward spiral for a very long time, when I met a woman who saw the light within me struggling to survive. She asked the angels what she could do to help me and they led her to her bookcase.

As she stood there in front of the books, *The Game of Life and How to Play It*, by Florence Scovel Shinn, *fell to the floor!*

So that's the book she loaned me.

What Florence had written over half a century before resonated deep within me and I took my power back! Immediately my energy shifted within to a higher vibration of love, joy and possibility. I reclaimed my power within and the experiences of my life shifted, too, creating miraculous prosperity left and right!

Only problem was... I would focus on Florence's principles, incorporating them into my life creating miracles - like finally meeting the love of my life, landing my dream job, receiving a 250% increase in pay, 5 weeks paid vacation, flexible hours and a new car - not to mention a wonderful sense of peace within! Then I'd get caught up in the tasks and responsibilities of every day living and I'd revert back to old habits of struggling in fear.

Then... Miraculously... *The Game of Life* would appear again in my life! I discovered that no matter where I opened the book, it was as if an unseen hand guided my fingers; because the powerful, magical energy of the words on the page would speak to me, supporting me, giving me strength to shift my energy from deep within to the higher vibration of love. I would implement Florence's teachings and I'd be catapulted into the land of miracles!

On my own I had made living in some form of fear an art form, then Florence's teachings changed all that - I took my power back and learned that I deserve to be happy! AND... that I have the power to create the highest possible outcome as my experience - consistently.

Life flowed into spiritual work with an open connection to the angelic realm. Therefore I was very open to working with the spiritual energy of Florence when in 2006 her energy came to me in spirit form. She wanted me to write an e-course based on *The Game of Life*. Of course I said, Yes! What a GREAT idea! When we began, she chose which chapter to work on and when we released the finished e-course to the Soul Kisses community - *they loved it!*

Then in 2009 Florence came back and wanted me to convert the e-course to a workbook and self-publish it - like she did back in 1925. Just how fantastic is that? Another Brilliant Idea by Florence! So we put the manuscript together and self published *Florence Scovel Shinn's Game of Life ~Unleashed~* - and the Soul Kisses community *loved it!*

I worked closely with Florence, writing the e-course and workbook, but I'm still human... and I found that maintaining my higher vibration of creation energy to consistently create the life I wanted to live.... still slipped sometimes and I would create life experiences I really didn't want.

Good GRIEF!

How could I master transforming this pattern? What did I need to do to stay in the energy I wanted to BE in as much as humanly possible?

The answer was, I needed support - human support. I work with my angelic team all the time, but I needed a human to help me hold the space of tangible support in order to expand and direct my creation energy consistently in order to fulfill my version of heaven on earth. So I reached out and got the support I needed. I learned how to stop the energy drain and maintain my energetic focus with the highest vibration of love possible as my "Normal" way of BE-ing ---- *consistently.*

If I can shift my life that was once ravaged with fear, working in jobs where I was underappreciated and underpaid, kissing frogs to find my Prince Charming, feeling separated from God and alone and turn that all around from a disappointing life to a life I LOVE - ***you can too!***

The GAME of LIFE Mastery Program

If you need a human hand for tangible support to fully expand into the life you came here to live, and you love the simplicity of Florence's teachings, your next step is The Game of Life Mastery Program based on *The Game of Life Workbook!*

Devorss & Company was the first publisher to pick up *The Game of Life* after Florence self-published almost 100 years ago. In February of 2011, Devorss asked to publish the workbook Florence and I wrote. We took it off the market, re-formatted it, then in January of 2014, the all new Game of Life Workbook hit the bookshelves. On January 28, 2014, it became an international best seller at Amazon - selling out in the US, Canada, France and Germany! I watched Amazon sell out LIVE in the US - 3-2-1- Sold Out!

In March of 2014 we presented the first Game of Life Mastery Program and participants excelled at diving into winning their game of life!

The Secret introduced people to their internal power, but The GAME of LIFE Mastery Program based on *The GAME of LIFE WORKBOOK* teaches you ***how to access*** your internal power and direct it to create desired results: more loving relationships, optimal health, increased cash flow, work you love and everything in between!

PLUS the program holds a surplus of Dynamic Mastery Tools to help you transform the resistance energy that blocks you from experiencing the joy that is your birthright to experience.

I invite you to join us for the next GAME of LIFE Mastery Program! As of the printing of this book, all students get a LIFETIME Membership to the GAME of LIFE Mastery Program.

To learn when the next mastery program begins, so you won't miss out, go here on the web:

www.TheGameOfLifeMastery.com.

www.SoulKisses.com

The Secret Door to Success MASTERMIND

If you're looking for a smaller, intimate, interactive community of loving support based on this book, then The Secret Door to Success MASTERMIND is for you.

When the angels brought to me the concept of this mastermind, they showed me the energy of it and it was *Amazing.* Then with Florence's energy, the angels and I presented and the energy far exceeded my expectations. It was nothing short of miraculous.

Together we hold the space of unconditional love creating a safe container to be heard and supported like never before. We became a family of loving support that we all long for.

Each student broke through the barriers that had been holding them back all their lives and they created miracle after miracle.

I invite you to join us for the next Secret Door to Success MASTERMIND!

To learn when the next mastermind begins, and have your name added to the list, go here on the web:

www.MySecretDoorToSuccess.com

www.SoulKisses.com

In love and light,

Kate

PRAISE FOR the Secret Door to Success MASTERMIND

Dear wonderful Kate,

It is hard to put into words how incredible I think you and your programs are, but I will try!

After participating in the Game of Life Mastery Program and experiencing tremendous spiritual and personal growth, I was extremely excited to take part in The Secret Door to Success Mastermind. This program is truly incredible and I can honestly say I am a different person (in a very, very good way!) than I was before I started.

Kate Large is an extremely gifted spiritual guide and teacher. She truly cares about her students and her love and support is the secret ingredient that makes her programs have such power. I feel truly blessed to have found her and her programs and teachings.

I have been on a spiritual path most of my life, turning to God for help to survive an abusive childhood and then an unhappy, unloving marriage. I struggled with low self esteem and low self worth and feeling not good enough and undeserving.

Kate and the other amazing people who were part of the mastermind with me created a safe, loving supportive space for me to heal and grow.

This program is so amazing because as I sit here with tears in my eyes, I know this program and Kate's love and wisdom has truly Healed My Soul.

Parts of me I didn't even know were broken are now healed and whole and I look at life through new eyes, with a loving, positive outlook.

I have changed from a person filled with fear and desperation, hoping and praying something would finally change, to a strong woman who Knows she is the Master Creator of her own life and all that I desire is Mine! Moving from hoping and wishing to true knowing is an invaluable gift and I will be forever grateful to Kate and all the people who I now consider my dear friends who did the program with me.

Search your heart, if you are led to this program, you will be truly amazed at the powerful positive changes it will invoke within you. Take the chance, you are worth it and I assure you Kate will not let you down!

Kate, I mean every word - when we joined the SDS Mastermind, you promised we would create a manifesting blueprint that we could use for the rest of our lives - you completely fulfilled your promise! You are a such a blessing. Thank you for everything.

With love and gratitude,
Amy
South Carolina, US

Hello Beautiful Kate,

I cannot thank you enough, Kate, for creating and leading the Secret Door to Success Mastermind with such loving guidance.

When a small group of people come together to master material and chart their own particular course with it, it is invaluable to have a leader and guide like you.

Your understanding of (and ability to communicate) the nuances of Florence's work, and your support of the mastermind members as they build their confidence and begin to manifest on their own are cornerstones of the success that comes from being a part of this mastermind.

I have now truly mastered living my Heaven on Earth!

For those who are finally ready to truly shift their reality through implementing the work of Florence Scovel Shinn, with your loving and inspired support, this is the only mastermind program to consider!

Sending you love, light, blessings and cyber hugs...
Patti
Canada

Dear Kate

It is with much appreciation and pleasure that I write this testimonial having participated in your first Secret Door to Success Mastermind Program.

At the very start of the journey, you promised that we would learn how to create our own manifesting blueprint, and that we could/would use it for the rest of our lives. You absolutely were true to your word and really fulfilled your promise!

There were so many aspects to creating the blueprint, which is an empowering document, that changes as we grow and expand energetically in all areas of our lives that we want to use it for. Truly inspiring!

The support and love from the other gals in our group is stunning! Even though our mastery program has officially ended, we all stay connected via calls and our private Facebook Community, and my partner/buddy (from the program) and I enjoy our ongoing weekly calls. This has been instrumental in achieving all that we set out to do.

Thanks again Kate for everything .. so appreciative of your leadership, gifts, love and support!

Love and blessings
Pam
Australia

Dear Kate,

This amazing program has help me to focus and face issues I was afraid to look at. With the loving support of Kate and the group, it helped me feel not alone. The teachings have touched me deep inside and reconnected me to my spiritual beliefs.

All my life I have wanted a loving family who would hear me and support me to be the greatest expression of ME possible. I never dreamed I would get it from a virtual program, but I did! Kate and the angels held the safe space for each of us to be vulnerable and heal our painful wounds of the past so that we can now be Empowered to powerfully create the life we've dreamed of.

This program is life changing and I highly recommend it.

Lots of Love,
June
Connecticut, US

My lovely Kate.

You asked for us to send you information on our experience with the Secret Door of Success Program. I sat down and thought, how am I going to do that? How can I put my feelings into words? My words would seem empty to the experience and feelings that I have about the program and what I experienced.

When you first advertised the program, I sighed with relief because I knew that God and the Angels were listening.

From the moment I received the Secret Door to Success: Your Manifesting Blueprint book I felt the surge of hopefulness that vibrated from the pages. I knew I was about to change my life and the way I looked at it. I was able to experience the magnitude of feelings and steps to create my heaven on earth!

I was always looking for the "How". The "How" to change my life because I was really tired of being in the same place, living from the same thought process that I have had my whole life.

With this program I experienced the following:
1. Letting Go – Learning how to let go and that it is safe
2. Learning to come from a place of love
3. Trusting the knowledge that I have inside myself - this has been HUGE for me!
4. Being part of a group of incredible women that have become my lifelong friends
5. New ways to recognize and release what no longer serving me

The transformation I have been able to encounter with this program is life changing!!!! I have been able to manifest a new position with an increase of 15%, incredible benefits and the ability to work from home a couple days a week to be home with my daughters. I don't feel that I would have been able to do that without Kate and her program.

If you are ready to change your life sign up for Kate's program to create your heaven on earth!

All my love,
Pam
Indiana, US

Dear potential mastermind family member,

The angels told me they wanted me to present the Secret Door to Success MASTERMIND just before Christmas 2015 - and they wanted me to do it in January. Really? The book, The Secret Door to Success: Your Manifesting Blueprint, hadn't been written yet!

Then they showed me the energy of the program - OMG ===> it was MAGICAL!

The energy was magical and intoxicating and expansive and ascended my vibration to a level I'd never experienced before - and we hadn't even started yet!

Then on January 26th, 2015, the new Secret Door to Success family met for the first time - virtually by phone/Skype - and I discovered the angels had only given me a glimpse of how truly magical coming together with these ladies would be.

Time and space ceased to exist as the angels held the loving space for the six of us to gather at our manifesting round table.

We were heard like we've never been heard before - vulnerable without being vulnerable - seen as the beautiful goddesses of love and light that we are - always fully supported in a loving space that defies description by the human word.

Amy, Patti, Pam, June and Pam bravely opened their hearts to the love that they are and illuminated the fear that had been hidden there to see it for the illusion it is. With clarity they created their personal blueprint for manifesting the joy filled life they deserve now and always.

If you are interested in being a valued member of something bigger and greater than you are - something that ascends your energy and transforms your life, please contact me so I can answer your questions and secure your seat at the manifesting ro und table.

In deepest, sincerest gratitude and love,
Kate
Founder, The Secret Door to Success: Your Manifesting Blueprint MASTERMIND

PRAISE FOR the GAME OF LIFE Mastery Program

Prior to *The Game of Life* finding its way to me, I had worked for a few years with a spiritual counselor (1995-2001) which gave me a great foundation. I've been successful in my life in many regards however, I can see that I have placed limits on myself based on past upbringing and ingrained beliefs.

In 2008 I enrolled in a 1 year mentor program with Bob Proctor. I developed a better understanding of how to "play the game of life" in just two months with *The Game of Life Workbook* than after one year in Bob's program.

I've read a lot and followed a lot of people and I'm not sure if anyone can explain the game of life, which we each play, as simplistically as Florence does. I think it's impossible to use the word "Florence" and "complicated" in the same sentence.

The Game of Life Mastery program has been a fantastic experience for me. I believe I was lead to meet Kate, and when given the opportunity to study with her I didn't think twice. Kate took me from where I was in my spiritual journey before the program to a new level. She put my spiritual growth on steroids, through her kind and caring explanations to her guided meditations, to move me closer to my spiritual and life goals. I was skeptical anyone could teach me the steps I needed to rid myself of worry. Yet Kate's step-by-step guidance did wonders for me. I met my personal "worry angel" (Simon) and handed over my worries to him. Does this mean I'm worry free? No, I just now know how to purge my worries quickly. In addition, I've noticed a great diminishing of worries in my life since meeting my "worry angel."

Kate is not afraid to share her personal experiences, of her own spiritual journey, which creates a comfort in approaching her and asking the questions you might think are trivial; but you find are not. Another aspect of this program that just blew me away was the amount of bonus material she shares with each participant. You will find Kate is unselfish in pouring out her resources to support your spiritual journey and growth.

Dominikija Prostak

****

During a class module I was having trouble with my computer and couldn't get on the call. When I read the transcript I was thrilled to discover that as I read it, the loving energy that I receive on the calls was also very strong when I read the transcript! As a Lifetime Member, every time I experience the course, I get more out of it. I'm getting just what I need each time I participate. Thank you, thank you, thank you.

Barbie C.P.

****

I was desiring to go deeper in studying and applying metaphysical principles in my life, when I came across the Game of Life Mastery Program. I watched the introductory videos and used the gift meditations provided by Kate. I had such a shift from just the videos that I signed up for the program.

Kate has taken the timeless teachings of Florence Scovel Shinn and added tools to support your study. I can feel the healing energy of love in Kate's voice and her guided meditations are amazing. Although there is a lot of material, I did not feel overwhelmed as Kate encourages everyone to go at their own pace and listen for guidance. Taking the Game of Life Mastery Program was one of the best decisions I made this year. And I plan to take it again next year.

Catherine Rose Stevens, Intuitive Consultant, Energy Healer, and Spiritual Coach

www.YourHealingPathways.com

****

Your teachings have blown me away. I have been on a spiritual path for so many years, most recently focusing on learning to work with my angels. I have books, recordings, articles, paid readings and have learned a lot. But I have never had so many strategies presented to me as you have done. All of the meditations, processes, strategies, and guest speakers address different aspects of life. The affirmation information took the concept to a whole new level. All of the love and forgiveness activities are ones I am using.

There is so much information that I still have not processed it all. Your love and compassion comes through in each lesson. Sharing your own difficulties was so helpful as I struggle and feel that I must be the only one that struggles.

And to top it all off, I can do the program again as a lifetime member. Often, online classes present a lot of information at a fast pace to take it all in. It will be valuable for me to do the class again.

I took the class because when I read Florence's book, it blew me away. I knew the concepts from my other work, but she had a way of expressing them so simply, but powerfully, that I couldn't put her book down. So when you offered the class, I knew I had to take it. I didn't know what to expect, but I got way, way more than I ever dreamed.

God bless you.

Mary Jo Cox

****

Twenty years of intense personal development and growth have made significant positive changes in my life and yet, the Game of Life Mastery Program with Kate Large has helped me to reach a whole new level.

While Florence Scovel Shinn's teachings are simple, it can be a challenge implementing them consistently in our lives on our own, especially when we are facing trials and tribulations.

Kate's loving instruction, expansion of Florence's teachings and support of everyone in the Game of Life Mastery community are phenomenal!

If you're looking for that elusive 'something' to finally help you create (and live) the life of your dreams, the Game of Life Mastery Program is for you!"

Patti Smith, Money Mindset Coach

www.AwesomeWealthyWoman.com

****

As someone experiencing the Game of Life Mastery Program for the first time, I am already anticipating enrolling in the next available series....a wonderful advantage of the lifetime membership offered by Kate and her Mastery Team. This amazing course is so rich with materials and concepts that I feel I am only skimming the surface of what is available to a seeker of spiritual growth and enlightenment.

According to a Buddhist proverb: "When the student is ready, the teacher will appear." I believe this expression epitomizes my involvement with Kate.

For most of my life, I have been searching for my true purpose and gathering the courage to fully embrace what the child within me already knew when I came into this world - I was born to be a poet. A vocation of this nature is not readily endorsed by our Western society, so I often felt in my youth that I didn't quite fit into the mainstream of life. More significantly, however, I had a very well-intentioned father who simply wanted his children to have "real jobs". Therefore, I was strongly discouraged as a teenager from listening to my intuition and following my dreams. Consequently, I wandered through a variety of employment options, each one, in retrospect, being very valuable in the circuitous route of reclaiming my identity.

However, in the process of trying to find fulfillment in a variety of "real jobs", I suffered the alienation that comes from denying our spiritual essence. Although the "writer" within me inevitably surfaced in one way or another, I never fully declared who I was until about ten years ago. So I have many inner obstacles and resistances to overcome.

During the past decade I have been working specifically on this very process and I feel that Kate's program has come into my life at exactly the right moment. It is very exciting to realize that each time I explore the insights of Florence Scovel Shinn, as expanded upon by Kate, I can look forward to an ever-increasing awareness of my divinely-ordained life plan.

I eagerly anticipate each week's class module and have been learning to use the tools recommended for re-writing our neural pathways, clearing blockages, and claiming "what is mine by divine right under grace for the greater good of all". Early in the program I met my "worry angels" and the procedure for calling upon them has been very liberating. By attempting to live in the highest possible vibration of love energy, I know that I will become much more successful in attracting my vision of "heaven on earth".

Thanks to all the bonus gifts included with Kate's program, I now have a "cleanse and clear meditation" that I include as an important part of my daily exercises. Kate's angelic voice and exquisite visualizations have added significantly to my non-medicinal treatment for high blood pressure. A holistic approach to health has always seemed instinctively right to me. Therefore, I regard Kate as a powerful healer who brings a wealth of wisdom and skills to a world in great need of her superb mentoring. I especially appreciate the fact that Kate quickly responds to all our questions and works so diligently to ensure that her program not only meets but exceeds our expectations.

Another aspect of the program which has proven to be extremely supportive is the private Facebook community. I went from no Facebook affiliation prior to this program to suddenly experiencing a community of like-minded individuals who are beacons of light, sharing warmth and loving illumination.

Thank you, Kate, for bringing the brilliance of Florence Scovel Shinn to a new generation. Thank you especially for interpreting her ideas with the radiance of your light and love. And thank you for your belief in our ability to attract the abundance that is our birthright.

Sharon Sinclair

www.PoetrySpeaker.com

****

My a-ha moment was recognizing the many different types of emotions under the umbrella of "fear". I was able to shift with the tools taught to the love energy quite quickly. I could see the difference in my surroundings when I did this. I feel different too -- empowered - because I was able to recognize my fear and make a choice of HOW I want to feel, then shift it.

I have taken many different classes that were similar to this yet the energy of this class was different. The teachings took me to a different level of being. The teachings are simple yet profound. I would highly recommend this class! I am looking forward to being a Lifetime Member!

Divine Blessings,

Camille Pukay, Animal Communicator and Reiki Specialist

www.AnimalReikiDivine.com

****

I get the daily Soul Kisses and when Kate started using quotes from Florence Scovel Shinn, I checked her out on Google finding out this awesome progressive thinking woman was born September 24th … 1871!!! And self published *The Game of Life and How to Play It* in 1925. Amazing! When Kate put out the email about Mastering the Game of Life, I was interested but needed some reassurance before spending the money … it was definitely not in my budget plans.   I justified not registering by telling myself I would read the book and sign up 'next time'.

On the last possible day of registration I was still really on the fence! So I called on my angles. I asked them to send me a penny from Heaven if I was meant to sign up. And in case they needed an alternate option, they could show me some form of wings. This way I would know without a doubt what to do. I did see a couple of Harleys on the way home, but knew in my heart that was not my sign for this. After a stop at my Chiropractor I decided to stop looking and go get a haircut. As I crossed the street on the way to my car I happened to notice a glint on the pavement. Yep you guessed it, a brand new 2014 penny, face up giving me my nod to signup!

Well the program has been more than I could have imagined! Kate is truly interested in participants succeeding. The calls are recorded. Within 24 hours we had copies of the call and transcripts, meditations and other supporting materials. I have never had transcripts of any study course. For me, being able to listen to the calls again later allowed me to be fully in the moment during the live calls. The transcripts allowed me to make easy accurate notes of things important to me. Hearing, reading and writing helped me fully integrate what I'm learning.   My workbook is not pristine but filled with colorful highlighting.

Over the last several weeks I have pealed off a few more layers of my personal onion and 'got it' on a deeper level that all life's lessons are important. What I don't learn to navigate now will be patiently waiting for me at some future moment. Thanks Florence! Thanks Kate, for the life time study option. I have already signed up for the next session. Here's to Mastering the Game of Life with a smile :o)

Heather B.

****

I want to preface this by saying have engaged in spiritual seeking for over 20 years. I have read and tried to apply what I learned from numerous books such as "A Course In Miracles" and almost every book by Marianne Williamson, " Angelspeake", "The Secret", "Conversations With God", many books by Dr. Wayne Dyer like "The Power of Intention" and every book by Gary Zukav relating to "The Seat of the Soul". I also tried Gary Zukav's online Emotional Awareness course, all with limited and short lived success. I also tried the program "The Solution" by Laurel Mellin and read her book "Wired for Joy" and even had a one on one session with her.

So, I have tried and failed countless times. But, I did not give up and kept seeking. In August of this year during a dark and depressed period of my life, I meditated and prayed and pleaded for guidance and help from God and the angels, day after day. Then I saw an email in my inbox from Kate about the Game of Life Mastery program. It was for the second video, which I watched and immediately watched the first one as well.

As soon as registration opened I signed up.

I was, and continue to be amazed at how quickly things changed, the powerful breakthroughs I have experienced and the changes in me since starting the program.

All the things I tried before had good information and advice, but not much clear direction on how to implement it. Such as rewriting neural pathways, or "The Secret" saying you needed to be positive so think of something happy like a cute puppy and to try to convince yourself you already have what you want. But, when you are sitting in your crappy car and it won't start it is not easy to convince yourself you have that nice brand new vehicle.

Kate and The Game of Life Mastery program have truly changed my life. Many spiritual books say raise your energy to higher vibration, but do not tell you how to do that. Kate gives you an abundance of tools to accomplish this. She also provides clear guidance on how to work with your Angels for guidance and support.

The private Facebook page is also a tremendous support. Not only will others respond and support you, but Kate herself regularly responds, answers questions and gives you inspiration and warm, loving support.

What is the difference between The Game of Life Mastery Program and all the others I have tried? For me the most important difference has been Kate herself. I cannot emphasize enough how instrumental her warm, caring support is to succeeding at this program. I feel truly blessed to have found her and this program.

Also, I absolutely love the fact that she incorporates talking to your angels, and a focus on God as the creator of all that is, with the law of attraction principles. Everything she teaches such as rewriting neural pathways, talking to your angels and raising your energy to a higher level, I have read about and tried before, but until now could not do it.

I have made more progress since I started this program then in the previous more than 20 years of effort combined. Kate is an inspirational, motivational and effective teacher and leader of this wonderful program. If you are open and receptive, this program will change your life!

Kate thank you again for everything, and for your caring and support. You are truly and amazing person!

Amy Goguen

****

I first came across the writings of Florence Scovel Shinn when a friend gave me the book "The Magic Path of Intuition" as a Christmas present in 2013. I started to read it straight away and couldn't put it down .. I must have read it over and over on so many occasions .. I couldn't get enough of it.

I then researched online to see what other books Florence had written and came across the four-in-one book and it was ordered straight away by another friend of mine, who bought the book as a gift as I had re-introduced her to Florence's work and she also started putting things into action.

I further researched and came across Kate Large's Workbook on *The Game of Life and How to Play It* and ordered it straight away .. couldn't wait for it to arrive. When it did, I started using the Workbook immediately and noticed lots of shifts of energy and just felt like I finally found the right tools for me to create the life I wanted to have.

I had a couple of questions that I wanted answered and not knowing Kate (yet), I found an email address in the book and wondered if it would still be in existence .. so I sent an email with my questions, and to my very great and wonderful surprise, I received a reply from Kate herself, not only answering my questions, but also advising that if I had any other questions, please feel free to email her again .. I couldn't help but think what a nice person to offer that.

Kate very kindly sent me information about her Soul Kisses website and kindly gave me a complimentary invitation to attend her 5 day Mini Vacation with the Angels meditation she was running .. signed up for these and loved the meditations .. I noticed on Kate's website she was intending to run a Mastery Program on *The Game of Life* and so I signed up for it and couldn't wait for it to start. As I had been having such a shift in my energy and have been letting go of so many judgments, old non-serving habits, thought patterns etc and found myself in a much better place, so I invited a couple of my friends to also participate in Kate's Mastery Program and the three of us loved it and experienced so many wonderful aha moments ..

I am attracting in so many wonderful moments/opportunities and helping so many other friends with all that I have learned this year, I have been truly amazed with my progress. I know I am doing a lot of work on myself, however without Kate's guidance and love in my journey, I believe I wouldn't have progressed anywhere near as quickly as I have, nor appreciated or acknowledged my progress. Kate has supported me and is so accessible it is wonderful. I have done lots of programs with others, but never has the Facilitator been so accessible as Kate .. to me this shows she is true to her word and really wants to help spread the message about Florence's work.

In the Mastery Program, Kate has given us bonus sessions, we have had recordings and transcripts from the calls available within 24 hours, she has given away so many bonus gifts, introduced us to Mastery Experts and her generosity just keeps giving .. it is amazing!

If you are thinking about doing the Mastery Program, or perhaps having an Angel Reading with Kate, or doing any of her other programs, I would absolutely encourage you to go ahead and sign up! I'm so blessed I did and will be doing the Program again in the future .. I am shifting my energy and am creating in my life what I want to create .. I'm not where I want to be just yet, but I am so much closer to it than ever before and know it is about consistently moving forward, believing in myself, allowing my Angels to work with and for me .. it is a really exciting journey for sure!

Kate, thank you so much for your love, support and belief in me and for holding the energy for me to be who I came here to be, to create what I want to create and have everything I want .. I'm so appreciative and thankful and so excited about the journey forward.

Bless you Kate,

Pam F. (Australia)

****

Even though I've done so much of my own healing, The Game of Life Mastery Program illuminated areas and beliefs I'd kept well hidden. With each successive lesson, I dug increasingly deeper with the aid tools provided and the warm, encouraging support of Kate and my classmates. Each lesson allowed me to uncover something whether on my own or by hearing and being triggered by other students. I was amazed at how much more healing I needed and was THRILLED to do so right then & there!

This program helped me to shift out of old patterning, beliefs, attitudes, and habits that have been blocking me from living a full life. Sometimes the biggest hurdle is identifying the block or the false belief you've been carrying around deep, deep within! The gentle and loving acceptance of Kate and the other members of the class on the FB community and the use of provided tools allowed me to take risks in feeling through my old wounds and defenses to fully release that old emotional energy. I feel much lighter with increased feelings of peace and calm.

It's not 'magic' as you need to do the work and excavate your interior landscape but you learn to believe in yourself and own the power of your positive beliefs… in yourself and in the world/universe to support & provide for you. I have seen and experienced firsthand the power of my beliefs and the universe joining and creating synchronicities and events occurring for my highest good.

I love the book, *The Game of Life and How to Play It* by Florence Scovel Shinn, and the pure simplicity of it. Then, to have the benefit of delving in deeper to each lesson weekly with Kate was such a bonus. This book and this course are really timeless and I have found myself returning to both the book and lesson & tools again & again as other events arise in life AND finding solutions and further insights I didn't see the first time through the material. It truly is masterful at teaching me to 'retrain my brain' out of a fear & scarcity mindset to that of trust & abundance!

I highly recommend this course as it is life changing…from the inside out!

Dawn Pinke Anderson, Minnesota

Go to www.GameOfLifeMastery.com
and register to be notified when the next
Game of Life Mastery Program will be presented!

You've developed a momentum of energetic flow.
Set your intention to maintain this momentum to catapult you into and
sustain your new expression of BE-ing!

Continue your commitment to yourself to LIVE
your Biggest, Most Magnificent Life now and always!

www.ingramcontent.com/pod-product-compliance
Lightning Source LLC
Chambersburg PA
CBHW080555090426
42735CB00016B/3242